MY GREATEST
DAY IN BASEBALL

"You mean the day I'll never forget? That's easy, brother! We've only got to go back to 1941 when Brooklyn won the pennent. It was my first flag as manager, too, and I was fired before the day was over. Put that down in the books."

—LEO DUROCHER

"My greatest thrill in baseball didn't come from any ball I hit, from any base I stole or from any play I made. It came when I heard the national anthem played just before the start of the 1947 World Series, my first World Series."

—JACKIE ROBINSON

"Gosh, that was a great feelin' . . . gettin' a hold of that ball and I knew it was going someplace . . . yes, sir, you can feel it in your hands when you've laid wood on one."

—BABE RUTH

"I guess I've had more than my share of thrills from baseball, but the greatest game in my own book still stands as the one played on Friday the 13th of September in 1946 at League Park in Cleveland."

—TED WILLIAMS

**36 exclusive stories in one of the most unique
sports books ever written**

MY GREATEST
DAY IN BASEBALL

As Told to
JOHN P. CARMICHAEL

Sports Editor of the Chicago Daily News
and many other noted sports writers

GROSSET & DUNLAP • NEW YORK

CONTENTS

GROVER CLEVELAND ALEXANDER

as told to Francis J. Powers

> *Grover Cleveland Alexander, born February 26, 1887, in St. Paul, Nebraska, thrilled two generations of fans with his effortless pitching grace. He pitched the Phillies to their first pennant in 1915, and later came on to help the Cardinals to their flags of 1926 and 1928. In 20 years "Old Pete" compiled 373 victories in 686 games. Poor in health during his last few years, Alex passed away on November 4, 1950.*

My GREATEST day in baseball has to be the seventh game of the 1926 World Series between the Cards and Yankees. If I picked any other game the fans would think I was crazy. I guess just about everyone knows the story of that game; it has been told often enough. How I came in as a relief pitcher in the seventh inning, with two out and the bases filled with Yankees, and fanned Tony Lazzeri to protect the Cards' 3–2 lead. Actually, that was my greatest game, for it gave me not one, but three, thrills. But if it wasn't I'm stuck with it like George Washington with the hatchet.

There must be a hundred versions of what happened in the Yankee Stadium that dark, chilly afternoon. It used to be that everywhere I went, I'd hear a new one and some were pretty far-fetched. So much so that two-three years ago I ran across Lazzeri in San Francisco and said: "Tony, I'm getting tired of fanning you." And Tony answered: "Maybe you think I'm not." So I'd like to tell you my story of what took place in that game and the day before.

There are stories that I celebrated that night before and had a hangover when Manager Rogers Hornsby called me from the bull pen to pitch to Lazzeri. That isn't the truth. On Saturday, I had beaten the Yankees 10–2 to make the series all even. To refresh your memory on the series, the Yankees won the opener and we took the next two. Then the Yanks won two straight and needed only one more for the world's championship and I beat 'em in the sixth.

In the clubhouse after that game, Hornsby came over to me and said: "Alex, if you want to celebrate tonight, I wouldn't blame you. But go easy for I may need you to-morrow."

I said: "Okay, Rog. I'll tell you what I'll do. I'll ride back to the hotel with you and I'll meet you tomorrow morning and ride out to the park with you." Hell—I wanted to win that series and get the big end of the money as much as anyone.

Jesse Haines started the seventh game for us, pitchin' against Waite Hoyt. We figured Jesse would give the Yanks all they could handle. He was a knuckle-baller and had shut 'em out in the third game. Early in the game Hornsby said to me: "Alex, go down into the bull pen and keep your eye on Sherdel [Willie] and Bell [Herman]. Keep 'em warmed up and if I need help I'll depend on you to tell me which one looks best."

The bull pen in the Yankee Stadium is under the bleachers and when you're down there you can't tell what's going on out on the field only for the yells of the fans overhead. When the bench wants to get in touch with the bull pen there's a telephone. It's the only real fancy, modern bull pen in baseball. Well, I was sitting around down there, not doing much throwing, when the phone rang and an excited voice said: "Send in Alexander."

I don't find out what happened until the game is over. Haines is breezing along with a 3–2 lead when he develops a blister on the knuckle of the first finger of his right hand. The blister breaks and the finger is so sore he can't hold the ball. Before Rog knows it the Yanks have the bases filled.

I take a few hurried throws and then start for the box. There's been a lot of stories about how long it took me to walk from the bull pen to the mound and how I looked, and all that. Well, as I said, I didn't know what had happened when I was called.

So when I come out from under the bleachers I see the bases filled and Lazzeri standing in the box. Tony is up there all alone, with everyone in that Sunday crowd watching him. So I just said to myself, "Take your time. Lazzeri isn't feeling any too good up there and let him stew." But I don't remember picking any four-leaf clovers, as some of the stories said.

I get to the box and Bob O'Farrell, our catcher, comes out to meet me. "Let's start right where we left off yesterday," Bob said. Yesterday [Saturday] Lazzeri was up four times against me without getting anything that looked like a hit. He got one off me in the second game of the series, but with one out of seven I wasn't much worried about him, although I knew that if he got all of a pitch, he'd hit it a long piece.

I said okay to O'Farrell. We'll curve him. My first pitch was a curve and Tony missed. Holding the ball in his hand, O'Farrell came out to the box again. "Look, Alex," he began. "This guy will be looking for that curve next time. We curved him all the time yesterday. Let's give him a fast one." I agreed and poured one in, right under his chin. There was a crack and I knew the ball was hit hard. A pitcher can tell pretty well from the sound. I spun around to watch the ball and all the Yankees on bases were on their way. But the drive had a tail-end fade and landed foul by eight-ten feet in the left-field bleachers.

So I said to myself, "No more of that for you, my lad." Bob signed for another curve and I gave him one. Lazzeri swung where that curve started but not where it finished. The ball got a hunk of the corner and then finished outside. Well we were out of that jam but there still were two innings to go.

I set the Yanks down in order in the eighth and got the first two in the ninth. And then Ruth came up. The Babe had scored the Yanks' first run of the game with a tremendous homer and he was dynamite to any pitcher. I didn't take any chances on him but worked the count to three and two, pitching for the corners all the time. Then Babe walked and I wasn't very sorry either when I saw him perched on first. Of course Bob Meusel was the next hitter and he'd hit over 40 homers that season and would mean trouble.

If Meusel got hold of one it could mean two runs and

the series, so I forgot all about Ruth and got ready to work on Meusel. I'll never know why the guy did it but on my first pitch to Meusel, the Babe broke for second. He (or Miller Huggins) probably figured that it would catch us by surprise. I caught the blur of Ruth starting for second as I pitched and then came the whistle of the ball as O'Farrell rifled it to second. I wheeled around and there was one of the grandest sights of my life. Hornsby, his foot anchored on the bag and his gloved hand outstretched was waiting for Ruth to come in. There was the series and my second big thrill of the day. The third came when Judge Landis mailed out the winners' checks for $5,584.51.

I guess, I had every thrill that could come to a pitcher except one. I never pitched a no-hit game. I pitched 16 one-hitters during my time in the National League and that's coming pretty close, pretty often.

THE BOX SCORE
(October 10, 1926)

ST. LOUIS	A.B.	R.	H.	P.	A.	NEW YORK	A.B.	R.	H.	P.	A.
Holm, cf.	5	0	0	2	0	Combs, cf.	5	0	2	2	0
Southworth, rf.	4	0	0	0	0	Koenig, ss.	4	0	0	2	3
Hornsby, 2b.	4	0	2	4	1	Ruth, rf.	1	1	1	2	0
Bottomley, 1b.	3	1	1	14	0	Meusel, lf.	4	0	1	3	0
Bell, 3b.	4	1	0	0	4	Gehrig, 1b.	2	0	0	11	0
Hafey, lf.	4	1	2	3	0	Lazzeri, 2b.	4	0	0	2	1
O'Farrell, c.	3	0	0	3	2	Dugan, 3b.	4	1	2	2	3
Thevenow, ss.	4	0	2	1	3	Severeid, c.	3	0	2	3	1
Haines, p.	2	0	1	0	4	Adams	0	0	0	0	0
Alexander, p.	1	0	0	0	0	Collins, c.	1	0	0	0	0
						Hoyt, p.	2	0	0	0	1
						Paschal	1	0	0	0	0
						Pennock, p.	1	0	0	0	1
Totals	34	3	8	27	14	Totals	32	2	8	27	10

Adams ran for Severeid in 6th.
Paschal batted for Hoyt in 6th.

ST. LOUIS	0	0	0	3	0	0	0	0	0—3
NEW YORK	0	0	1	0	0	1	0	0	0—2

Errors—Koenig, Meusel, Dugan. Runs batted in—O'Farrell, Thevenow (2), Ruth, Severeid. Two-base hit—Severeid. Home run—Ruth. Sacrifice hits—Haines, Koenig, Bottomley. Sacrifice fly—O'Farrell. Struck out—By Haines 2, by Alexander 1, by Hoyt 2. Bases on balls—Off Haines 5, off Alexander 1. Hits—Off Hoyt, 5 in 6 innings; off Pennock, 3 in 3 innings; off Haines, 8 in 6 2-3 innings; off Alexander, 0 in 2 1-3 innings. Winning pitcher—Haines. Losing pitcher—Hoyt.

You know you think of a lot of funny things that happened in baseball, sittin' around gabbing like this. I remember when I was with the Cubs, and I was with them longer than any other club, we were playing the Reds in a morning game on Decoration Day. The game was in the 11th when I went up to bat and I said: "If they give me a curve ball, I'll hit it in the bleachers. My wife's got fried chicken at home for me." They gave me a curve and I hit 'er in the bleachers.

LOU BROCK

as told by Jack Orr

When Louis Clark Brock broke in as a Chicago Cub outfielder in 1962, it would have seemed highly improbable that he would emerge five years later as a World Series hero and the most effective St. Louis Cardinal offensive threat. He was fast, all right, but in other departments (hitting with consistency, throwing, catching fly balls), he was merely adequate. He changed all that with a determination that impressed the profession. Born June 18, 1939, at El Dorado, Arkansas, he was at the top of his form by 1967 and it was predicted that he would be the Cardinal left fielder for another seven or eight years. After that, he plans a career in insurance.

IN THE Cardinals' 1967 run for the pennant, Lou Brock hit .299, including 21 home runs, and stole 52 bases. But his teammates insisted that those figures were only half the story. Brock, as fast a man getting from first to second as the game has seen, made other contributions by so upsetting the rival pitcher that the Cardinals, as often as not, were able to snatch victories from losing situations.

This ability to turn a game around was never more dramatically displayed than it was in the 1967 Series against the Boston Red Sox. When Brock reached base, as he did in five of the seven games, it usually meant a Cardinal triumph. When he didn't reach base, St. Louis lost. "Our job," said

Red Sox manager Dick Williams, "is to keep that darned Brock from getting to first. After that, we can take care of the rest."

That was the way the Series worked out. Brock reached base 14 times in the Series (12 hits, 2 walks), scored 8 of the Cardinals' 25 runs, stole bases almost at will (7 in 7 attempts). Analysts of the classic agreed that more than any other Cardinal batsman, Brock was the one factor that scuttled the Red Sox hopes. The seven stolen bases broke a record involving one of the most hallowed of baseball figures: Honus Wagner, one of the original members of the Hall of Fame. Back in 1907, sixty years earlier, Jim Slagle of the Chicago Cubs stole six bases in a five-game series against Detroit. And Wagner, playing for the Pittsburgh Pirates, stole the same number in a seven-game Series against the same Tigers—and against the same catcher, Charlie Schmidt —in 1909.

From then until 1967, no one matched that total. When Pepper Martin became famous in the 1931 World Series by running the Cardinals of that day to victory over the Philadelphia Athletics, he stole five bases. Even Maury Wills, the Dodgers' premier base stealer of all time (104 in 1962), could only steal three bases in a single Series. Brock's 12 hits wound him up one short of the Series record, set by Bobby Richardson of the Yankees in 1964, and his eight runs in one Series had been exceeded only twice—once by Lou Gehrig and once by Babe Ruth.

Four of those Brock base hits came in the opening game, won by St. Louis, 2–1, and coupled with his two stolen bases, gave evidence of the handwriting that was to be on the wall for the rest of the October classic.

There were 34,796 fans on hand at Fenway Park that afternoon as Brock dug in as the lead-off hitter against Jose Santiago. Brock calmly stroked a single to center—and one pitch later stole second. He didn't score that time because Dalton Jones, the Sox' third baseman speared a sharp grounder and turned it into an inning-ending double play.

But in the third inning, when Brock got up again, he was responsible for the first run of the game. He singled up the middle, took a deep breath, and scampered to third on Curt Flood's double down the left field line. The run scored on an infield grounder by Roger Maris.

The Red Sox made it 1–1 when pitcher Santiago lifted a home run over the left field wall and that was the way things stood until the seventh.

Brock again led off in the Cardinal seventh. He ripped a single to center and on the second pitch stole second with a head-first slide. The throw from catcher Russ Gibson was high, and Brock's hand got to the base under shortstop Rico Petrocelli's tag. Petrocelli started to argue with umpire Frank Umont, but Umont, on top of the play, gave three quick safe signs and said, "No! No! No!" Petrocelli shrugged and walked away from the argument. Flood then advanced Brock perfectly by hitting a ground ball to the right side of the infield, one of the Cardinals' superb minor talents, and when Maris hit a grounder to Jerry Adair at second, Brock was across the plate almost before Adair fielded the ball. It marked the second time in the game that Maris had hit a grounder to the right side, enabling the speedster to get in from third.

Now with his four straight hits in the box score, Brock came up in the ninth with an opportunity to become the first five-hit player in Series history. By now John Wyatt was the Sox pitcher, and he carefully pitched to Lou, and as a result, walked him. Brock scampered merrily off first base and so flabbergasted the Boston pitcher that he balked— and Brock took second. He was stranded there as Flood and Maris went out, but there was no doubt where the hero's laurels belonged. Four hits, a walk, the only two runs scored, two stolen bases, a maneuver which forced the opposing pitcher to balk—and two fairly hard outfield catches combined to make it a day that Brock will never forget.

In the second game, Brock went hitless—and the Cardinals lost. In the third game, Brock got two hits, a triple on which he ran to third like a jet and a perfect bunt single, and scored two runs—and the Cardinals won. In the fourth game, Brock hit safely twice, leading off the game with a leg single that sparked a four-run Card inning—and the Cardinals won again. In the fifth game he was shut out— and the Cardinals lost. His contributions in game No. 6 were substantial—two hits, two runs and a steal—but Boston had its hitting clothes on and tied the Series at three games. Then came the final game and more Brock exploits. In the fifth inning when it was still a close 2–0 game in favor of St. Louis, Brock singled again and immediately stole

THE BOX SCORE
(October 4, 1967)

ST. LOUIS	A.B.	R.	H.	P.	A.	BOSTON	A.B.	R.	H.	P.	A.
Brock, lf.	4	2	4	2	0	Adair, 2b.	4	0	0	2	2
Flood, cf.	5	0	1	2	0	Jones, 3b.	4	0	1	2	2
Maris, rf.	4	0	1	3	0	Yastrze'ski, lf.	4	0	0	4	1
Cepeda, 1b.	4	0	0	6	0	Harrelson, rf.	3	0	0	0	0
McCarver, c.	3	0	0	11	2	Wyatt, p.	0	0	0	0	0
Shannon, 3b.	4	0	2	0	1	cFoy	1	0	0	0	0
Javier, 2b.	4	0	2	1	1	Scott, 1b.	3	0	2	8	0
Maxvill, ss.	2	0	0	2	2	Petrocelli, ss.	3	0	0	0	0
B. Gibson, p.	4	0	0	0	0	dAndrews	1	0	0	0	0
						Smith, cf.	3	0	1	1	0
						R. Gibson, c.	2	0	0	8	0
						aSiebern, rf.	1	0	1	0	0
						bTartabull, rf.	0	0	0	1	0
						Santiago, p.	2	1	1	0	0
						Howard, c.	0	0	0	1	0
Totals	34	2	10	27	6	Totals	31	1	6	27	5

```
ST. LOUIS   0 0 1  0 0 0  1 0 0—2
BOSTON      0 0 1  0 0 0  0 0 0—1
```

ST. LOUIS	IP.	H.	R.	ER.	BOSTON	IP.	H.	R.	ER.
B. Gibson (Winner)	9	6	1	1	Santiago (Loser)	7	10	2	2
					Wyatt	2	0	0	0

Bases on balls—Off B. Gibson 1 (Scott), off Santiago 3 (Maris, McCarver, Maxvill), off Wyatt 2 (Maxvill, Brock). Struck out—By B. Gibson 10 (Adair 2, Jones, Petrocelli 3, Smith, R. Gibson 2, Santiago), by Santiago 5 (Flood, McCarver, Gibson, Javier, Cepeda), by Wyatt 1 (Javier).

aAnnounced for R. Gibson in seventh. bRan for Siebern in eighth. cGrounded out for Wyatt in ninth. dFlied out for Petrocelli in ninth. Runs batted in—Maris 2, Santiago. Two-base hits—Flood, Scott. Home run—Santiago. Stolen bases—Brock 2. Sacrifice hit—Howard. Double plays—Jones and Scott; Jones, Adair and Scott. Balk—Wyatt. Passed ball—R. Gibson. Left on bases—St. Louis 10, Boston 5. Umpires—Stevens (AL) plate, Barlick (NL) first base, Umont (AL) second base, Donatelli (NL) third base, Runge (AL) left field, Pryor (NL) right field. Time—2:22. Attendance—34,796.

second and third and ambled home on an outfield fly. Those two steals tied the Series record and when he walked against Dave Morehead in the ninth and swiftly stole second, the new mark was set.

At the end of each Series, it is the custom of a sports magazine to award a new Corvette automobile to the outstanding player of the Series. After much soul-searching, the editor tabbed three-game-winner Bob Gibson as the recipient, but the St. Louis radio station which broadcasts Cardinal games felt so strongly about Brock's contributions that it matched the award and Brock also received a new auto.

Brock's acquisition by the Cardinals from the Cubs in 1964, in exchange for ace pitcher Ernie Broglio, was at the time considered a steal for the Cubs. But Broglio never again was a big winner and the steal, if it was one, was the addition of the fleet Brock to the Cardinal starting lineup. Brock's hitting improved in St. Louis, his fielding and throwing picked up and he learned how to bunt and also hit the long ball.

His greatest forte, though, was his remarkable knowhow and speed in stealing bases (74 in 1966, 52 in 1967). He studied rival National League pitchers with an intensity. He became the best in the majors, even outstealing the fabled Maury Wills by 23 successful swipes in 1967.

But the day he remembers best, the day he impressed the nation with his magnificent hitting, running, stealing and opportunism remains that opening games of the 1967 World Series when he did everything his most avid fans could ever hope for.

DEAN CHANCE

as told by Jack Orr

A farm boy from Wooster, Ohio, Wilmer Dean Chance, born June 1, 1941, grew into such a tremendous high school pitcher that he won 51 out of 52 games, 18 of them no-hitters. He was signed by the Baltimore Orioles, who somehow let him slip away to the Los Angeles Angels in the expansion draft. There he became the best pitcher in baseball, winning the coveted Cy Young Award, at the tender age of 23, with a won-lost record of 20–9 and an incredible earned-run average of 1.65, the lowest in almost a quarter of a century. He followed with two disappointing seasons, was traded to Minnesota for the 1967 campaign and he again became a 20-game winner, for which he was honored as the Comeback Player of the year. His post-baseball ambition: Back to farming in Wooster, Ohio.

DEAN CHANCE blossomed into a great major league pitcher with astonishing suddenness. In his first two years with the new Angels, he lost one more game than he won (28–27). And things didn't look promising when 1964 came around. At the time of the All-Star break that year he was still only 5–5, though he was named the American League starter, pitching two-hit shutout ball for his three innings.

Then Chance went to work with a vengeance. He compiled a 15–4 record over the second half of the season and pitched 12 complete games. His earned-run average over this stretch was 1.64. Overall, he pitched 11 shutouts, struck out

17

107 batsmen, hurled five two-hitters, one three-hitter, four four-hitters and four five-hitters. But still it was no easy matter to win for Los Angeles in those days; their hitters were next to last in league averages and if they got him two runs, it was a bundle.

So Dean had to do it the hard way. He pitched 11 shutouts to lead the majors, and six of those were by 1–0 scores, the toughest kind of a grind for a pitcher in this era of pop-fly, lively-ball home runs. Nobody else in history ever had won half a dozen 1–0 games in one season. Besides, he beat the ultimate champions of the league, the Yankees, four times without a loss, and in 50 innings pitched, allowed the Bronx Bombers just one run, a homer by Mickey Mantle. There was hardly a dissenting vote when Chance was named the best pitcher in either league.

It was a great off-season for Dean. He had joined up with Bo Belinsky, reputed to be a playboy, and they went on a pool-shooting tour that winter. In addition, there were the traditional baseball banquets held to honor the game's newest star.

There may be no connection between the expansive life Dean was living and what was to follow. But for whatever the reason, he had two (for him) rather so-so years. In 1965, he won 15 of 25 decisions and his earned-run average almost doubled. In 1966, he slipped further to 12–17. By now, the Angels had moved into a spanking-new stadium in Anaheim, California, and had changed their name to the California Angels.

Dean's reversal of form had made him the American League's most intriguing enigma. Though he had suffered minor injuries in 1965 to offer some kind of excuse, Chance's arm was perfectly sound the following year. Still he continued to lose. Manager Bill Rigney theorized that Dean was pressing too hard and his arm tightened. Pitching coach Marv Grissom shrugged and said, "I still think he's capable of throwing a shutout every time he starts. If I knew why he doesn't, I'd retire a millionaire." Chance's inconsistency continued, as did the Angels' hitting. The team average was .232, next to last again.

So the club decided it needed hitting more than it needed a question-mark Chance and a deal was made. The Angels gave up their onetime ace to the Twins in exchange for sluggers Jimmy Hall and Don Mincher and relief pitcher

Pete Cimino. The trade did little to help California, which finished fifth, but it worked wonders for the Twins, who had a chance for the pennant up until the very last day of the season.

Chance was the Chance of old. Early in the year he was pitching at a sensational pace of nearly a strikeout an inning. In June, after he beat his old teammates, the Angels, in an easy 7–2 game, his record was 7 victories in 8 decisions, and by All-Star time, he was 11–7, with three of his defeats by a single run. He again started for the American League in the 1967 All-Star contest, giving up two hits and a run in three innings. The Nationals won in the 15th, 2–1.

Along the way, Dean seemed to get back his confidence— "cockiness" was the way his rivals described it—and as the Twins continued to stay in contention, his pitching became more effective. He also seemed to have calmed down on the extra-curricular scene. Instead of Bo Belinsky as a running mate, Chance teamed up with his roomie, rookie Jim Ollom, a quiet, confident type not given to the type of escapade Belinsky became known for. (Belinsky played for the Houston Astros and had a 3–9 year.)

The highlight of Chance's comeback year came late in the season against the Cleveland Indians. He pitched his first no-hit game in the majors, though a month earlier he had pitched five perfect innings against the Red Sox in a game halted by rain.

The no-hitter was something of a novelty because the Indians had scored a run in the first inning on two walks, an error and a wild pitch. But Chance refused to let it bother him as he struck out nine and hung tough through the last eight innings. His mates tied the score in the second and went ahead in the sixth, 2–1, and with that lead, Chance whistled through the final three innings. He took the back-pounding by his fellow Twins in stride and wasn't even ruffled when the clubhouse phone rang and it was a long-distance call from Vice-President Hubert Humphrey, a Minneapolis buff, who called to add his personal congratulations.

"He was loose as a goose all the way," said pitching coach Early Wynn in describing Chance's greatest feat. "He was very calm. Though we didn't mention the no-hitter through-out the game, he knew what was going on. Sometimes we talked over the hitters coming up in the next inning. There was no tension in his eyes or face. He was all business."

By year's end, with Minneapolis missing the pennant by one game to the rampaging Red Sox on the final Sunday, Chance's comeback was a reality. He had rebounded from his worst major league season to the charmed 20-win circle. He had extended his career 1–0 victories to twelve, eighth highest in the history of the game. And he had pitched a hitless game.

Back home in Wooster, Ohio, Chance found that the prices on hogs he sells had almost doubled during 1967. So had Dean's chances, at 26, of becoming one of the game's pitching superstars in the years ahead.

THE BOX SCORE
(August 25, 1967)

MINNESOTA	A.B.	R.	H.	RBI.	CLEVELAND	A.B.	R.	H.	RBI.
Carew, 2b.	5	0	1	0	Maye, lf.	2	1	0	0
Uhl'nder, cf.	4	0	1	0	Davalillo, cf.	3	0	0	0
Tovar, 3b.	4	1	1	0	Hinton, rf.	3	0	0	0
Oliva, rf.	3	1	2	0	Horton, 1b.	4	0	0	0
Killeb'w, 1b.	3	0	2	1	Alvis, 3b.	3	0	0	0
Val'spino, lf.	4	0	0	0	Azcue, c.	3	0	0	0
Zim'rman, c.	3	0	0	0	Fuller, 2b.	1	0	0	0
Hern'dez, ss.	3	0	0	0	Whitf'ld, ph.	1	0	0	0
Reese, ph.	1	0	0	0	Gonzalez, 2b.	0	0	0	0
Versalles, ss.	0	0	0	0	Brown, ss.	3	0	0	0
Chance, p.	3	0	0	0	Siebert, p.	2	0	0	0
					Wagner, ph.	1	0	0	0
					Culver, p.	0	0	0	0
Totals	33	2	7	1	Totals	26	1	0	0

```
MINNESOTA    0 1 0 0 0 1 0 0 0—2
CLEVELAND    1 0 0 0 0 0 0 0 0—1
```

MINNESOTA

	IP.	H.	R.	ER.	BB.	SO.
Chance (W. 17-9)	9	0	1	1	5	9

CLEVELAND

	IP.	H.	R.	ER.	BB.	SO.
Siebert (L. 6-11)	8	7	2	2	2	7
Culver	1	0	0	0	1	0

E—Tovar. DP—Minnesota 2, Cleveland 1. LOB—Minnesota 8, Cleveland 3. 2B—Carew. HBP—By Siebert (Chance). WP—Chance, Culver. Balk—Siebert. U—Napp, Umont, Kinnamon and Valentine. T—2:48. A—10,519.

TY COBB

as told to Francis J. Powers

A proud man to the day he died, Ty Cobb's proudest achievement was his being given the most Hall of Fame votes ever. A unanimous choice on virtually every all-time All-Star team ever assembled. Cobb held a fistful of records, including games played, times at bat, runs scored, stolen bases. In the latter department he led the American League six times and his record of 96 for the year 1915 stood until 1962. He was the Detroit Tigers' greatest player, and finished with a lifetime batting mark of .367. He played until he was 42, maintaining a strong interest in the game until he died July 17, 1961.

THERE WAS little brotherly love toward the Detroit Tigers when our club arrived in Philadelphia on the morning of September 27, 1907. That old city was baseball mad; it was mad at the Tigers and very mad at me. The wildest race the six-year-old American League then had produced was nearing an end and the Athletics were leading the Tigers by a half game. It had been a four-way race all summer with the defending White Sox, Athletics, Tigers and Cleveland jumping in and out of first place. Now the chase had boiled down to a fight between the Tigers and Athletics and would be settled in the series which was to open the next afternoon. For there were only two series remaining for each club.

The Tigers had come fast that year to be pennant contenders. Hughie Jennings, famous shortstop of the old Baltimore Orioles, had been brought up to manage the team and his "E-yah!" and grass-picking had made him a popular figure. I was on my way to winning my first batting championship and running the bases well. We had tremendous power with Claude Rossman on first and Sam Crawford in center field and I think those Tigers really were the first of the great slugging teams that later made the American League synonymous with power. We had some great pitchers but particularly Wild Bill Donovan, one of the finest men ever in the game, who won 25 games and lost only four that season. Ours was a fighting team that neither asked nor gave quarter, patterned after the old Orioles of Jennings and John McGraw.

Philadelphia resented us as upstarts, for Connie Mack still had much of the same team which won the 1905 championship and then had lost to the Giants in that famous World Series where every game was a shutout. The Mackmen had sensational pitchers in Chief Bender, Eddie Plank, Rube Waddell and Jack Coombs and were a solid defensive team. They were hot to reclaim the championship they had lost to the White Sox the previous season.

We won the first game of the series on September 28, when George Mullin outpitched Chief Bender, and went into first place by a half-game. Then it rained and a double-header was scheduled for September 30. There was the pennant. If we won, we had only Washington and St. Louis ahead while the Mackmen had a series with Cleveland before getting to the Senators and the "Naps," as Cleveland was called in those days, were certain to give Philadelphia trouble.

When we went on the field to start play there were 30,000 fans looking on. There were 25,000 packed into old Columbia Park that had a capacity of 18,000, and the rest were crowded into windows and on the roofs of houses overlooking the field. There were fans, several rows deep, around the outfield, restrained by ropes and mounted police, and they weren't the least bit friendly. Before that afternoon was finished and we left the park in the autumn dusk with street lights aglow, I had experienced about every thrill that can come in baseball . . . or so it seemed to a 19-year-old boy.

Jennings picked Donovan to pitch for the Tigers, leading

with our ace, while Mr. Mack started Jimmy Dygert, a spit-baller. Mack had Eddie Plank, the southpaw who always was tough to beat, ready but decided to save him for the second game. You never saw and maybe never heard of a game like this one. It went 17 innings and took three hours and 50 minutes to play. It produced great pitching and poor pitching, long crashing hits and some of the most unusual incidents to be found outside the realm of fiction.

At the end of five innings, Philadelphia led us 7 to 1. The Athletics wasted no time in pounding Donovan. Topsy Hartsel opened with a single and stole second. Socks Seybold walked and Kid Nicholls sacrificed. Harry Davis' hit bounced off Charlie O'Leary's leg and into "Germany" Schaefer's hands but Seybold was safe at second and Hartsel scored. Murphy beat out an infield hit and then Seybold scored on Jimmy Collins' fly and Rube Oldring sent Davis home with a double into the crowd.

Jennings would have had any pitcher other than Donovan out of the game before that inning finished but Philadelphia was Bill's home town and his dad and relatives always came out to see him work so Hughie never took him out there. It looked like foolish sentiment at that moment, but proved to be a good policy three hours later.

For a few minutes in the second inning it seemed as if we would get them all back. Rossman singled and was safe at second when Dygert threw wild, after fielding Bill Cough-lin's smash. Charlie Schmidt sacrificed and then O'Leary hit to the box. Dygert chased Rossman almost to the plate before throwing to Ossie Schreck and then Claude hit the Athletics' catcher so hard he dropped the ball. Dygert walked Donovan but then Rube Waddell came in, and with a pitch that broke from your waist to the ground, fanned the next two batters.

The Athletics got two more in the third, Davis hit a home run in the fifth and Collins and Oldring hit into the crowd for another score and there we were, behind six runs. But this Tiger team was a fighting team and we moved back into the game with four runs in the seventh. Two walks and an error filled the bases and then Crawford drove into the left field crowd for two bases. Another scored on my infield out and Crawford raced home while Murphy was making a great play on Rossman. Then we were only two runs behind. The Athletics scored one in their half but we scored in the eighth and went into the ninth still two runs behind.

That ninth is one inning that always will remain bright in my memory. Crawford was on first when I came to bat and I hit a home run to tie the score. Right then and there Mr. Mack forgot about saving Plank for the second game and Eddie rushed to the box and retired the next three batters. We went out in front in the 11th when I hit into the crowd after Rossman's single but we couldn't hold the lead and the Athletics tied it, largely because of a wild pitch, at 9-all.

Then the game settled down to a brilliant duel between Donovan and Plank but at the same time produced some of the greatest confusion ever seen on any field. In the 14th inning, Harry Davis hit a long fly to center field that Sam Crawford muffed and it was good for two bases. Our team claimed interference, for a policeman had stepped in front of Crawford as he was following the ball along the ropes. "Silk" O'Loughlin was umpiring behind the plate (there were only two umpires in a game at that time) and it was his play. Both teams gathered around O'Loughlin, arguing and snarling. Finally O'Laughlin called to Tommy Connolly, umpiring at first base: "Was there interference?" Without hesitation, Tommy called: "There was." So Davis was out and that was lucky for us, since Murphy followed with a single.

During the argument with the umpires, Rossman and Monte Cross, one of the Athletics' reserve infielders, threw some punches and soon there were players and policemen all over the field. Rossman was tossed out of the game and that started a new argument. Ed Killian, a left-handed pitcher, finished the inning at first base and later Sam Crawford came in from the outfield to play the bag. After the game, Connie Mack was bitter in his denunciation of O'Loughlin and it was one of the few times when he really roasted an umpire.

There was no further scoring, although I got as far as third in our half of the 17th, and at the end of that inning the game was called with the score still 9-all. There was no second game that day; it never was played and the tie meant the championship for us. We left Philadelphia a half game in front and swept through Washington. The Athletics lost one to Cleveland and another to the Senators and we cinched the pennant in St. Louis . . . Detroit's first since 1887, when it was in the old National League.

Although I had the thrill of hitting the homer that tied the score and making two runs, the star of that game was Bill Donovan. I don't recall a similar exhibition of pitching in my 25 years in the American League. Bill allowed eight runs in seven innings and only one in the next 10 and fanned 11. The modern generation doesn't remember Donovan, but there was a pitcher with great speed, a great curve and a great heart.

The Athletics made 20 hits that day to our 15 and we had 17 runners left on base to their 13. They made six errors, so during the long afternoon there was just about everything to be found in baseball.

THE BOX SCORE
(September 30, 1907)

DETROIT	A.B.	R.	H.	P.	A.
Jones, lf.	7	1	1	5	0
Schaefer, 2b.	9	1	3	3	6
Crawford, cf.-1b.	8	2	2	7	0
Cobb, rf.	8	2	3	1	0
Rossman, 1b.	7	1	2	13	2
Killian, 1b.	0	0	0	1	0
Mullin, 1b.	1	0	0	0	0
Downs, cf.	1	0	0	2	0
Coughlin, 3b.	7	0	0	1	3
Schmidt, c.	1	0	0	3	1
Payne, c.	6	0	1	9	1
O'Leary, ss.	8	1	2	3	1
Donovan, p.	7	1	1	3	7
Totals	70	9	15	51	21

PHILADELPHIA	A.B.	R.	H.	P.	A.
Hartsel, lf.	9	1	4	3	0
Nicholls, ss.	6	1	2	4	9
Seybold, rf.	6	2	1	1	0
Davis, 1b.	8	3	3	19	1
Murphy, 2b.	7	1	4	2	6
J. Collins, 3b.	7	1	1	3	3
Oldring, cf.	7	0	3	3	0
Schreck, c.	4	0	0	9	1
Powers, c.	3	0	0	4	0
Dygert, p.	0	0	0	0	0
Waddell, p.	4	0	0	1	0
Plank, p.	4	0	1	2	1
E. Collins	1	0	1	0	0
Totals	66	9	20	51	21

E. Collins batted for Oldring in 17th.

DETROIT	0 1 0 0 0 0 4 1 2 0 1 0 0 0 0 0 0—9	
PHILADELPHIA	3 0 2 0 2 0 1 0 0 0 1 0 0 0 0 0 0—9	

Errors—Schmidt, Nicholls, Oldring, Schreck, Powers, Dygert (2). Two-base hits—Crawford, Cobb, O'Leary, Hartsel (3), Nicholls, Davis, J. Collins, Oldring (2). Home runs—Cobb, Davis. Hits—Off Dygert, 1 in 1-3 innings; off Waddell, 7 in 7 2-3 innings; off Plank, 7 in 8 innings. Sacrifice hits—Schmidt, Crawford, Nicholls (2), J. Collins, Powers. Stolen bases—Coughlin, O'Leary, Cobb, Hartsel. Left on bases—Detroit 17, Philadelphia 13. First base on balls—Off Donovan 3, off Dygert 1, off Waddell 1, off Plank 2. First base on errors—Detroit 4. Hit by pitcher—By Plank 1. Struck out—By Donovan 11, by Waddell 7, by Plank 3. Wild pitch—Donovan. Time—3:50. Umpires—O'Loughlin and Connolly.

DIZZY DEAN

as told to John P. Carmichael

Born January 16, 1911, either in Lucas, Arkansas, or Holdenville, Oklahoma, as Jay Hannah or Jerome Herman, he was, from 1932 through 1937, baseball's brashest, cockiest and "winningest" pitcher. This was the period of the Gas House Gang of St. Louis and Dean was a charter member. In 1934 Dizzy won 30 games, the last pitcher to reach this total, but arm ailments at the peak of a fabulous career closed out his active days as a member of the Chicago Cubs in 1941. After a successful run as a local and national baseball broadcaster, Dean retired to become a prominent figure on the sports banquet circuit.

As MIGHT have been expected, Jerome Hanna Dean did not confine himself to the traditional "Greatest Day in Baseball." He said: "I've had too derned many big days . . . lots of 'em."

I just wish my arm was like it was back in thirty-four. . . . I'd have me a picnic in this league. When I came up every club had three-four .300 hitters who really could powder that ball. Now? Shucks! I'd breeze home any day. I never forget Frank Frisch the day I beat Detroit 11–0 in the last game of the World Series in 1934. We're in the clubhouse, see, celebratin' and I got a rubber tiger, all blown up, and I'm twistin' his tail and hollerin' like the rest and Frisch came by and stopped and you know what he said?

"Anybody with your stuff should have won 40 games this year instead of a measly 30," he said. "You loaf, that's the trouble. Thirty games! You ought to be 'shamed of yourself." Imagine that, and me just winning the Series for him: ol' Diz out there pitchin' outta turn too, don't forget that. He wanted me to pitch although he'd said that Bill Hallahan was gonna work the last game. But he came to me the night before and he asked: "Diz, you wanna be the greatest man in baseball?" I told him I already was, but he didn't even hear me I guess, 'cause he went on: "You pitch that game tomorrow and you'll be tops." I just told him: "Gimme that ball tomorrow and your troubles are over." He wanted me to pitch I knew that. Hell, I was afraid he would let Hallahan start.

That was a big day in my life, I admit it. First World Series and all the excitement and everybody wild, and two trucks goin' up and down the streets, one playin', "Hold That Tiger" and the other tootlin' the "St. Louis Blues." I saw Babe Ruth and got his autograph, by jingo, and 'taint everybody pitches in a big series and gets Babe's name on a ball too. I liked that ol' Frisch, he was a helluva guy, but he worried all the time. He had nothin' to fret about with ol' Diz out there. You know we was leadin' 11-0 in the ninth with one out and he sent four pitchers down in the bull pen to warm up.

So help me, I thought they must be gettin' ready for the 1935 season. Eleven-nothing I got 'em and that Billy Rogell on base and Hank Greenberg came up. I already struck him out twice, no trouble 'tall, and when he came up in that ninth I hollered over to the Tiger bench, I said: "What, no pinch-hitter?" and Hank looked at me like he'd a liked to break one of them sticks over my head, but hell, he was my meat. He was easy.

You know what that Frisch did? I put two fast balls right past the letters on that Greenberg's uniform and when he missed the second one I hadda laugh. I put my glove up to my face to keep from laughin' right in his face, he looked so funny, and before I could throw any more Frisch came out. He was mad. He said: "Cut out the foolin', we got a lot at stake" and I just stood there and looked at him like he must be outta his mind . . . me leadin' 11-0 with one out in the last of the ninth. Just then Leo Durocher came in from short and he said: "Aw, what the hell,

Frank, let the guy have his fun. What's the matter with you?" Well you know what Frisch told me? Yeah . . . he said: "You lose this guy and you're through." Eleven-nothing . . . I can't get over that yet. He was gonna pull me.

That Greenberg couldn't a hit that next pitch if he'd a started to swing when I wound up. Gonna pull me. He didn't even see it and the next guy was Owen and he forced Rogell and the whole thing was over. Them Tigers weren't bad; they gave us a good battle, but they were just pussycats with me. I don't like to brag a lot, because folks think I'm a big lunkhead or somethin', but when I had my fast ball, before I broke my toe and couldn't throw it any more, nobody hit me . . . much. You know what I did one day? I pitched a game in Boston and never took a sign or never threw nothin' but fast balls. A whole game, Bill Delancy was catchin'. I told Al Spohrer, the Braves' catcher, before the game that he could tell everybody I was gonna do that too. I beat' em 10–0 or 13–0 . . . some score that. Just wound up and fogged that ball over.

I'll tell you another day in Boston I got a helluva kick. Remember seein' a big fat guy around with me a lot? Well, he was Johnny Perkins and he worked in a night club around St. Louis and he made this trip with us. He made me a bet I wouldn't strike out Vince DiMaggio the first time he came up. I did and when I went back to the bench I made motions to Perk I'd double the bet the next time. I struck him out again and I put everything back on a third bet and I fanned him three straight times. Then Perkins wanted to make it all or nothin' so I took 'im and when DiMag came up again he lifted a pop foul back of the plate. I thought Ogrodowski was gonna catch it and I ran and hollered: "Let it go, let it go." He couldn't get the ball anyway, as it turned out, 'cause it hit the screen, but I'd a bumped him sure as hell if he'd a got under it. I wanted to win that bet. I struck DiMaggio out next pitch . . . four straight times.

I got a great kick outta the time I was traded to the Cubs, just before the season opened in '38. All ballplayers want to wind up their careers with the Cubs, Giants or Yankees . . . they just can't help it. Seems like they're finally in the big time, although of course the Cubs used to pay derned good wages too, which they don't any more, so you couldn't help a guy wantin' to land there. I didn't know anything about it until I came in from the bench during a game with the Browns right in St. Louis . . . spring series, you know . . . and I was walkin' in the clubhouse door and somebody grabbed my arm and it was Clarence Rowland, 'cept I didn't know him then. He said: "Well, Diz, you belong to us now . . . you're a Cub." Hell, I thought he was a fan and kiddin' me and I said: "I'll see you later, bud," and went on inside.

There was a lot of newspapermen and photographers there and I wondered what was going on, but never dreamed a deal for me, and finally Branch Rickey came in and he whispered: "I want to see you in my office after you're dressed," and I said O.K., and then he called for silence and said: "We just want to say we've made a deal with the Cubs and we have traded this man here . . ." and he put an arm on my shoulder, but he should a put it under me 'cause I thought I'd faint . . . "and we don't want you players to feel we're letting you down, because we've got a man to replace him and we'll still win the pennant."

Well, nobody seemed to know who that man to take my place was, but "Pepper" Martin, he got up on a chair, with a towel around him . . . he'd just come from the shower . . . and he made a helluva speech. He sounds like Mr. Rickey at that. I'd hate to have to listen to both of 'em in the same night. They'd have a guy really dizzy and I ain't kiddin'. He said: "Mr. Rickey, we appreciate you coming in to tell us what you've done and that we ain't going to be too bad off even if Diz here goes, that you still want us to win a pennant and we're all for you and we'll win too." Hell, I knew they couldn't win any ol' pennant without Diz, even if I was only a half a pitcher then, so when they asked me to say something for the newspapermen I said: "Well, Mr. Rickey, I predicted we'd win that flag right here in St. Louis, but now that I'm gone, we'll win it in Chicago and I'll see you get into the World Series." How about that, huh, and then we back into it in Chicago? I reminded ol' Branch about that many a time, but I hadda laugh like the devil, 'cause we just made it.

That game I beat Pittsburgh in 1938 (Sept. 27) was just about as big a day as I ever remember. I never had nothin'. I wasn't even supposed to pitch. I was on the inactive list or somethin' and Gabby Hartnett came in the clubhouse that day and you know he twirls that big seegar around in that red face of his (I like ol' Gabby, even if I did call him a pickle-puss in Wichita which he was because he bawled me out right in front of all the players and people a-gazin' at me and fined me $100) and he said: "Dean, you're the pitcher" and I said: "Fine," but I thought he was kiddin' and then Larry French and Herman and them said: "He ain't foolin' Diz . . . you're pitchin'." My God, I couldn't break a pane of glass and I knew it, but I pitched.

They finally had to get me outta there in the ninth and I was leadin' 2–0 and Bill Lee went in and the first pitch he made was a wild one and a run scored, but he hung on and they didn't score again and, boy, I felt like a million. Ol' Diz saved many a game for Cardinal pitchers in his day and here was a guy who saved one for me and I told him, I said: "Lee, you're a great man," and he was a helluva guy and a swell pitcher. I always liked old Gabby, but he shouldn't have yelled at me in front of all those people in Wichita. They was a-gazin' at me like I was a freak and I don't stand for bein' shown up by nobody. The fine was all right. . . . I didn't get in until 20 minutes to 2 and we had a midnight deadline . . . but he could-a told me on the quiet.

The first game I pitched for the Cubs that year I beat Cincinnati and afterwards some of us went out and had a few beers and such, but I just went along. I didn't know what rules the Cubs had and figured these guys must know what they're doing. We had a helluva time, too, and then I beat the Cardinals and it looked like I'd have a great year, but Diz just didn't have so much left, I guess. But Mr. Wrigley told me not to worry, that he wasn't sorry he bought me and just go ahead and do the best I could and it's too bad I couldn't-a been with the Cubs when I wuz in my prime, because we'd a never got beat and I'd probably been drawin' $50,000 a year and pitchin' my arm off.

How about the time I had the run-in with Ford Frick? I'll never forget that either and I never apologized and never signed a derned letter and his secretary must-a wrote 20 different copies or somethin' for me to sign and I wouldn't. I was in a tough spot, though. See, I wuz pitchin' against Carl Hubbell here in St. Louis and he beat me 4–1. I led into the sixth or seventh and then George Barr, the umpire, called a balk on me; he said I didn't come to a stop before

I threw. He was nuts, but anyway they got three runs and ol' Diz never liked to take a beatin'. No time. So I had to go to Belleville, Ill., that night to a banquet . . . promised a friend of mine there . . . and they said I said Frick and Barr were a couple of crooks. 'Course I was still pretty sore by then, too.

That was pretty strong and the Cardinals were goin' East, and when we got to Brooklyn there I was suspended without pay and supposed to apologize. Frick had me up there and waved a lot of telegrams and said this was something terrible, look what all these people had to say, and I told him: "You must live out there and wait till I get some telegrams where I live" and I got some too and they all said I never said nothin' like he was a crook and I wouldn't sign no paper, but I was in a helluva spot and don't you forget it. Frisch was crazy. I got so many laughs listenin' to him I wouldn't a signed even if I'd been wrong and once I told him I had a notion to sue the National League for slander and Frank hit the ceiling. All he wanted me to do was get back in uniform.

So Frick finally saw the error of his ways and I got back, but I had a great time not workin' for a few days. Night-clubbin' every night and a couple of times I ran into ol' Frisch and gave him a big cheery hello and I didn't pitch neither until I made sure I got paid for that time out. Well, it was June 9, 1936, when I put on the uniform and Hub-bell'd beaten me May 19 in St. Louis. So here we were again and that Polo Grounds was a madhouse. I was afraid to come out of the dugout. Everybody was yellin' and throwin' things down at our bench and I waited until Frisch said: "You only got five minutes, you better warm up," so I dashed out there by home plate and warmed up and I was almost deaf from the noise when I got through.

I just went out there and pitched a cool three-hitter in the first game of a double-header and beat Hubbell 8–1 and I'd had a shutout only Durocher booted one near the end. Yes sir, ol' Jay Hanna Dean was just in ripe form that day and there was nobody gonna make a monkey outa him. I told that Durocher after the game, I said: "You oughta been more careful on that ball, I wanted to rub it in" and he said: "You rubbed it in enough, don't worry about it . . . the time to boot 'em, if you have to, is when you got runs to spare," which I guess is probably right.

Oh say, I'm forgettin' just about the best day of all, although there was nothin' like that Series of 1934, but the afternoon I struck out 17 Cubs wasn't no ordinary day neither. That was July 30, 1933, and nobody's broken the record yet. Frisch had only been manager a couple of days . . . he took Street's job . . . and Guy Bush started against me and nothin' ever occurred to me 'bout this bein' a big day. Hell, Koenig doubled and Herman singled in the first inning and I was losin' 1–0 'fore we ever came to bat. Frisch had two guys warmin' up . . . he didn't know ol' Diz so well then.

We had the biggest crowd in two years in Sportsman's Park, almost 30,000, and I came in off the bench the end of the first inning and Frisch said: "I'm sendin' you to the bull pen next inning if you don't get better" and I told him: "Hell, you worry about gettin' a couple of runs. . . . I just didn't warm up good." Well, Bush was the only man I didn't strike out on the whole Cub team. I didn't know nothin' about it, understand, 'cause I was just a-pitchin' away and Jimmy Wilson was catchin' and he never said a word and neither did anybody else. Hell, I might-a broke the record for consecutive strikeouts if somebody'd told me what I was doin', just like I could-a pitched a no-hit game in Brooklyn that time Paul did, 'cept nobody said nothin'. We'd a had a double no-hitter and no brothers ever did that before.

I struck out three men this day in the fifth and the eighth and ninth. Twelve of the 17 swung too at the last one. I never bothered with pitchin' high or low when I was good. . . . I just poured that ball in there, right over the plate. Koenig, Cuyler, Demaree, Hendricks and Jurges each struck out twice and I got that Babe Herman three times. He came up the fourth time and I just threw easy-like and he popped up for a change and he threw his bat away and yelled at me: "You must have a Bible in your pocket, you lucky bush so-and-so" but I didn't. It wuz only ol' Diz on one of his good days. If I'd known I was anywhere near a record I'd a struck out 20 anyway. . . . I just toyed with Bill Jurges a couple of times, figurin' he couldn't hit nothin' anyway.

Never forget the last inning. I struck out Hendricks and Jurges and that made it 16, I found out afterwards. Charley Grimm was makin' faces over on the bench and growlin' at me about bein' a big, dumb Oklahoma busher . . . hee-hee, I never forget he yelled at me: "You look like you live in one of those Oklahoma penthouses". . . you know what that is, a pigpen with Venetian blinds, and I almost got laughin' and spoiled it all. He sent up somebody named Mosolf to pinch-hit and ol' Wilson met this guy before he got to the plate and I could hear him say: "This is a helluva place to stick you in, kid. . . . I wouldn't be surprised if the first one this dizzy moron threw was right at your ear. He don't like pinch hitters."

Mosolf never took his bat off his shoulder. Wilson'd give me the sign and then he'd straighten up and pound his glove right behind Mosolf's ear and the guy thought surer-'n-hell he was gonna get punctured and I just put three through there. Dean specials with the smoke curlin' off 'em. You'd a thought we won the World Series the way everybody pounded me on the back in the clubhouse and told me what I'd done and I was pretty proud too. But hell, there ain't no use in me tryin' to talk about a special day, 'cause every time I had a ball in my hand, and that suit on, it was my greatest day. The only time you ever feel bad is when you gotta quit.

And with every rose must grow a thorn. "I'd a given anything in the world to have beaten the Yanks that time," said Dean, referring to the World Series game in 1938, with the Cubs, when he led 3–2 into the eighth. "I didn't have nothin'. I had no license to beat anybody. But they could-a cut off my arm in that clubhouse if I'd a won that one. Diz just stubbed his toe one year too soon, in that All-Star game."

JOE DiMAGGIO

as told to Fred Down

*Joseph Paul DiMaggio, the famed "Yankee Clipper,"
was born November 25, 1914, and was a product of
the San Francisco sandlots, like so many other diamond
greats. Hampered by injuries during a brilliant career,
he nevertheless made the Hall of Fame shortly after he
became eligible in the balloting. In 1941 he established
one of baseball's great marks, hitting safely in 56 consecutive games. He was selected Most Valuable Player
three times before he hung up his pin-stripe flannels
for good following the 1951 season. DiMaggio was
spring-time batting coach for the Yankees for many
years after his retirement. Then, after the 1967 season,
when Charles O. Finlay moved his Athletics from
Kansas City to Oakland, California, Joe was hired as
executive vice-president of the new franchise.*

I'D BE a heel if I didn't list October 1, 1949, as one of the
greatest days a baseball player ever knew. It was a day on
which the fans chose to honor me. And before it was over
I had a lump in my throat the size of Ted Williams' batting
average.

It was assumed that the American League pennant race
would be over when the day was picked originally. It wasn't,
of course. We were one game behind the Red Sox with two
to play. We had to beat them twice and they had their two
best pitchers ready to throw at us.

It would be folly to attempt to list all the things the fans

gave me. And it would not be fair to list some and leave
others out. The record speaks for itself. There must have
been one hundred presents. I wouldn't attempt to estimate
their value in money. Whatever that might be they had a
greater value.

My mother and family occupied a box seat behind the
Yankee dugout and I couldn't help thinking of them while
Mel Allen, who was the master of ceremonies, reeled off
presents and tributes to me. I couldn't help thinking, too,
of my teammates. They had stood up all season despite
70-odd injuries. I knew every man was certain the Red Sox
were not going to "steal" the prize from us at the very
end and I knew every man was waiting impatiently for the
game to begin.

I like to think that the long delay caused by "my day" did
not affect their play. I cannot be sure of that, of course. There
must have been many times when they thought, "Come on,
give the guy his presents and get on with the game. There
is a pennant to be won."

Maybe they would have won that game more easily if
there had been no "Joe DiMaggio Day." But it was enough
to me—and I think to them—that they did win. Joe Page
came on to stop the Red Sox cold for the last six and one
third innings. The race was tied and we went on to break
the tie once and for all the next day.

That, then, was one of my "greatest thrills." Ted Williams
says he would rather win the batting title than gain the most
valuable player award because the title is something you earn
yourself and the most valuable award something which someone gives to you. I realize what he is driving at. But I would
not trade any batting title I ever won for that day which the
fans gave me.

I'd have to consult the record book to tell you when I won
the batting title. But I'll never have to check the book to
tell you about those 70,000 fans who came to Yankee Stadium
that day for the express purpose of honoring me.

There was another crowd on another day which I'll never
forget either. Which brings me to my "other greatest thrill."

This one is not as easy to tell you about. It is always simple
to tell about the homers you hit and the games you won. It
is more difficult to talk about the strikeouts and the defeats.
Especially when you try to explain the thrill in it.

For the record the day was Sunday, October 3, 1948. The

setting was Fenway Park in Boston. The crowd was about 31,000 and it had come to see Yankee blood.

We could no longer win the pennant. Jack Kramer had beaten us, 5 to 1, the day before. It was between Cleveland and Boston with Cleveland leading the Sox by one game. The Red Sox could gain a tie and force a play-off by beating us providing Cleveland lost to Detroit. So those 31,000 fans were watching two games that day—one on the field and one on the scoreboard.

We had nothing except satisfaction to play for. You might say there must have been a let-down in our play. But there wasn't. It is never fun to lose. Besides, the league standings did not convince us that there were two better teams in the league. Maybe we were wrong but that's the way we felt. And we thought we could go a long way toward proving our point by beating the Red Sox that day.

Well, the game is history. We got a run in the first inning when I doubled but the Sox rocked Bob Porterfield for five in the third. Joe Dobson was their pitcher but he wasn't too sharp and I knew we'd get him sooner or later.

My family was in the stands and I know they were rooting for the Red Sox. They knew I couldn't play in the World Series no matter what happened but Dom had a chance if the Sox won and Detroit beat Cleveland. And there was the score after three innings on the board—Detroit, 5, Cleveland, 0.

But Dobson was faltering and we got him in the fifth inning. Phil Rizutto singled and Bobby Brown doubled. Then I hit one off the left field wall. That cut the margin to 5 to 4. The crowd was really going crazy.

My mother told me later that my sister Marie almost went crazy too.

"What is he trying to do?" she screamed. "Doesn't he want Dom to play in the Series?"

The fact is that I probably didn't at that moment although I rooted for him the next day in the play-off.

I had charley horses in both legs and the one in my right leg hurt like fury. I know I couldn't have gone much further. I was happy that it was the last game of the season. But I wanted to stay in there. To win on the last day, if possible.

We didn't, of course. They beat us, 10 to 5. And I didn't last all the way. Bucky Harris sent Steve Souchock in to run for me after I got my fourth hit—a single—in the ninth.

I saw Souchock come out of the dugout and trot toward first.

"Bucky says you've had enough," he said.

I turned and started for the dugout. I guess I was limping pretty badly. Anyway that's what they told me later.

I'll never forget that crowd. It was standing and roaring—like one man. I tipped my cap but it didn't stop. I looked up at the stands and I never saw a more wonderful sight. There were 30,000 people giving an ovation to a guy who had tried to beat them. They were still yelling when I disappeared into the dugout; they didn't stop for another three or four minutes.

Dom and I had a reunion after it was all over.

"Well," I said. "You did it. I hope you win tomorrow." He was looking at me kind of funny.

"That was the greatest tribute a crowd here ever gave a ball player," he said. "Everybody is talking about it."

"I guess you felt like cutting my throat when I hit that one off the wall in the fifth inning," I said. "I know Marie did."

"No," he said, and he was dead serious. "Don't ever tell Joe McCarthy this—but I felt like applauding too."

* * * * *

It wasn't difficult for me to single out that game in Fenway Park on the last day of the 1948 season as the greatest game I had ever played. After all that was the finish to one of my greatest seasons, one in which I had taken clear title to leadership in both the home run and runs batted in departments for the second time in my career, but just let me tell you about one game, rather one homer which furnished me with my most satisfying afternoon.

The 1950 season was about the longest I had known. I was in a slump from the opening bell and just did manage to untrack myself long enough in the last two weeks to push my batting average above the .300 mark, the second lowest in my career. For some a .301 average might indicate a pretty good year, but I was really below par throughout the campaign and when I did get my blows they came in bunches. It was far from a steady performance and if ever there was a hot-and-cold hitter that year, it was DiMaggio.

That we eventually won the pennant was no fault of mine.

I hadn't been of much help, and a little siege of virus (how that guy follows me around!) in mid-August sapped my strength and caused me to lose weight.

The Series began in Philadelphia, and we beat Jim Konstanty, 1–0, but I might just as well have stayed in the hotel, I did draw a couple of passes, but on my other two times up I hit a couple of infield flies which my son, Joe, could have snatched. And I was much worse the next afternoon—at least for a while!

Robin Roberts and our Allie Reynolds hooked up in a ding-donger and at the end of nine innings we were all knotted at 1–1, and my streak of popups continued unbroken. There were a couple of "wicked" floaters to Mike Goliat at second base, one to Willie Jones at third base, and a "screamer" to Eddie Waitkus at first base. Up and down they went, not even going beyond the grass which borders the infield. Four times at bat in this one, twice in the first game and I hadn't even driven a ball past the Phillie inner defense. I was really burning with rage at my pitiful demonstration and I don't think I hated a guy as much as poor Roberts when I came to the plate in the 10th inning.

The Phillie right-hander slipped behind in the count at 2-and-1, and I sort of anticipated his high, hard one at this point, the pitch which had kept me popping up. And Roberts didn't disappoint me! I rifled his next pitch, and I knew it was gone. Ever see one of those taut wires at the circus which extend from the ground to the highest perch? Well, that's how that ball traveled—right into the upper left-center seats for the game-winning homer.

There was no mistaking the happiest Yankee in the clubhouse a few moments later. You'd think I had just broken Babe Ruth's record, that's how big my smile was. I had finally smacked one, and I was tingling all over. No home run ever gave me such satisfaction!

LEO DUROCHER

as told to John P. Carmichael

With time out for a short stint as a radio broadcaster, the slightly incredible Leo Ernest Durocher has been part and parcel of the major-league scene since 1928. He came up with the Yankees, moved to the National League, achieved his greatest fame with the Dodgers of the '40s. He won two pennants with the New York Giants and his greatest managerial achievement was driving the Giants to four straight victories over the Cleveland Indians in the 1954 Series. Durocher also coached the Los Angeles Dodgers, which means he has appeared in World Series as a player, manager and coach.

In 1966 Leo again appeared as a major league manager when he took over the reins of the Chicago Cubs. They finished last that year, but in 1967 astonished the baseball world by making a serious run for the National League pennant for almost two-thirds of the season. They finished third.

YOU MEAN the day I'll never forget? That's easy, brother! We've only got to go back to 1941 when Brooklyn won the pennant. It was my first flag as manager, too, and I was fired before the day was over. That's right. Won a pennant and I was fired as manager the same day. Put that down in the books.

In the first place, I didn't think I'd live to get to Boston, where we clinched the flag. I couldn't sleep nights. If you recall we played a double-header in Philly the Sunday before and we won the first game easy and I was all set to let Curt Davis go in the second one, when Larry MacPhail came in the clubhouse and asked: "Who yuh workin' this game . . . Luke Hamlin?" I said: "No, Davis," and he didn't say nothin' and walked out.

Well I got thinkin' about Davis and Hamlin and whip-sawin' myself and finally wound up with Hamlin and Lit-whiler hit a homer off him with the bags loaded in the first inning and we blew it. I was afraid to shave that night because I couldn't stop shakin' and finally I went to a barber and I thought of Casey Stengel as I got in the chair; the time he dropped two in one afternoon, walked into a shop, sat down and told the guy:

"Once over and never mind cutting my throat. I may do that myself later in the evening."

That just shows you how things were going when we got to Boston for those two games. We won the first, thanks to "Dixie" Walker's three-run triple in the eighth, and that only made things worse. I didn't close an eye all night. "Peewee" Reese had booted one to give Boston the lead and I lay awake wondering if maybe I hadn't better take him out the next day and play myself. I got up outta bed four times . . . the last time at a quarter after 5 . . . and made out different lineups. Finally I just stayed up.

Oh, how that morning dragged. Every time I picked up a paper I read where if we won and the Cards lost we were "in" and then I'd have more coffee. It was a helluva relief to get into the uniforms; just putting it on seemed to quiet me a little and I'd keep telling myself, "What you worryin' for: Wyatt's pitching and he's beaten these mugs five straight times. He'll handcuff 'em." I remember as we were walkin' out on the field, ol' Whitlow came by and maybe he figured the skipper could stand some cheering up and he put a hand on my shoulder and said: "Get me one run today. They won't score!" That's all.

We got him one right off the bat. Walker singled, went to third on two infield outs and then Medwick topped a ball toward third. I saw it might be a hard play for Tom Early, the Boston pitcher, and hollered to Joe: "Run for your life." I thought afterwards that must have sounded funny as hell, because what else would he do, but anyway he beat the play by a step and Walker came home. In the next inning Owen was on second with two out and took third as "Dixie" singled again . . . too short for Mickey to score. But Walker got himself trapped off first and maneuvered around long enough to let Owen count before he was caught.

I was feeling a little better by then and so help me if that Rowell, at second, didn't make three straight errors in the third and give us another run. You'd a thought those guys were winning a pennant. They were so damn anxious to beat us, like everybody else in the league, and they blew up. He kicked Camilli's grounder, just an easy roller, and then threw it way and he fell all over Medwick's ball and Dolph scored from second. About the time Reiser hit that homer in the seventh to make the score 5 to 0, the guys in the press box were hollerin' down that the Cards were losing 3 to 1 and somebody on our bench let out a yip and I shut him up. It was too soon to shake hands with ourselves.

That Wyatt was beautiful to watch. They got three hits off him in seven innings and not a man reached third. I never said a word to him at any time, nor to any man on the club, except to yell and holler, "Keep the 'pepper' up." Whitlow was my best pitcher. If we couldn't win with him, the chances were we couldn't win at all. The same went for the whole team. There it was on the field, the best we had. The fourth hit off Whit came by Rowell in the eighth and they sent up Frank Demaree to pinch hit. He was ready and he hit one. I can close my eyes now and see Billy Herman going for that ball.

He made the (deleted by censor) stop I've seen in many a day. He just dove, almost full length, after it and still kept his feet. That was the end. We were home. I started to laugh, like a kid who knows Santa Claus is coming that night. Wyatt went through the motions in the ninth and we carried him into the clubhouse. It's funny to see big, swearing men cry, but they did. Everybody was tired and worn and happy.

That ride to New York was something! We had a special train. We drank up $1,400 worth of beer, Scotch and champagne on the trip. Well, you were on it . . . remember when Tony Martin, the movie guy, got up to make a speech and somebody hit him smack in the face with a hot steak? The gang yelled: "Sit down, you bum, this isn't your party," and from then on it was a riot.

At New Haven the conductor got a wire from MacPhail telling him he'd board the train at 125th Street in New York.

I didn't know anything about a wire, but the conductor came to me and asked if we wanted to stop there. I told him no. We knew there'd be a mob in Grand Central Station and some of the fellows wanted to get off at 125th and slip home, but I vetoed that. I told them: "I don't care if they tear your clothes off. We belong to those fans. They've been waiting 21 years for this chance to celebrate and we've gotta go through with it. There'll be no stop."

We went right on through. MacPhail was standing on the platform with Sam Breadon and Branch Rickey. They were on their way to see Rochester in the playoffs. We passed 'em up, just like that; went roaring right on and I got a glimpse of MacPhail and I said to myself: "Oh, oh, there'll be hell to

THE BOX SCORE
(September 25, 1941)

BROOKLYN DODGERS	A.B.	R.	H.	P.	A.	BOSTON BRAVES	A.B.	R.	H.	P.	A.
Walker, rf.	5	1	3	3	0	Sisti, 3b.	3	0	0	1	4
Herman, 2b.	4	0	0	2	2	Dudra, 3b.	1	0	0	0	0
Coscarart, 2b.	1	0	0	0	0	Cooney, c.	1	0	0	0	0
Reiser, cf.	3	1	2	2	0	Moore, cf.	3	0	0	0	0
Camilli, 1b.	4	1	0	10	0	Hassett, 1b.	4	0	0	9	2
Medwick, lf.	4	0	1	1	0	Waner, rf.	3	0	1	1	0
Lavagetto, 3b.	2	1	0	1	4	West, lf.	4	0	2	3	0
Reese, ss.	3	0	1	2	0	Miller, ss.	3	0	0	3	0
Owens, c.	4	1	1	5	0	Roberge, 2b.	0	0	0	1	0
Wyatt, p.	4	1	1	1	0	Rowell, 2b.	3	0	2	2	0
						Berres, c.	2	0	0	5	2
						Johnson, p.	0	0	0	0	0
						Earley, p.	2	0	0	1	3
						Masi, c.	1	0	0	1	0
						Demaree	1	0	0	0	0
Total	34	6	9	27	6	Totals	31	0	5	27	11

Demaree batted for Berres in the 8th.

BROOKLYN	1	1	1	0	0	0	0	2	1	0—	6
BOSTON	0	0	0	0	0	0	0	0	0	0—	0

Errors—Miller, Rowell (3). Runs batted in—Medwick, Reiser (2). Two-base hit—West. Home run—Reiser. Stolen base—Owens. Double plays—Herman to Reese to Camilli, Hassett to Miller to Hassett, Miller to Rowell to Hassett, Johnson to Miller to Hassett. Left on bases—Brooklyn 7, Boston 5. Bases on balls—Off Wyatt 1, Earley 5, Johnson 1. Struck out—By Wyatt 5, Earley 5, Johnson 1. Hits—Off Earley, 8 in 8 innings; Johnson, 1 in 1 inning. Losing pitcher—Earley. Umpires—Reardon, Goetz and Stewart. Time—2:08. Attendance—10,096.

pay about this." There was. I met him in a Hotel New Yorker elevator. He never said a word. Didn't congratulate me or the team or a thing; just looked at me. We got off at the same floor, walked into the same suite together, never talked.

People began to come in and he called me into another room. Still didn't say anything about the pennant. "Why didn't you have the train stopped at 125th?" he shot at me. I told him I didn't know he'd sent a wire; I told him why we decided to go on through, so the players wouldn't get off. He was plenty mad. Told me I might have called him up and asked and a lot of junk and finally I said I was runnin' the team, not the (deleted by censor) train and he barked back:

"Well, you're not even runnin' the team any longer. You're fired!"

So I said "all right" and walked out and went up to my own room. Somebody sent up word the newsreel men were waiting below and I refused to come down. I never did, either. They had to use Joe Medwick and I never saw the pictures afterward. Maybe they didn't use 'em. I stayed where I was and finally went to bed. I was so tired I coulda slept standin' up. About 3 o'clock in the morning the phone rang and it was MacPhail.

"You comin' by the office in the morning?" he asked.

Twice as mad now, because I'd been asleep, I yelled into the phone: "What for, to get my money?" and hung up. In about two minutes it rang again.

"No," he said, "I want to talk over some things about the series with you." I said: "Okay," and went back to sleep.

That's it!

BOB FELLER

as told to Ed McAuley

One of the game's undisputed mound greats, Bob Feller had an appreciable dent put into his career by four years of active Navy service in World War II. He wound up with a total of 266 victories, might have pushed the 400 mark had his career remained uninterrupted. Possessor of a half-dozen series marks, Feller pitched three no-hitters, and a dozen one-hitters. Feller's hallmark was his blazing fastball. At its peak of efficiency it was good enough to strike out a record total of 348 batters in 1946. He is now a successful insurance executive in Cleveland and a member of the Hall of Fame.

I CAN truthfully say that I've never thrown a baseball in anger. For one thing, my tendency toward wildness has kept me concentrating as calmly as possible on the business at hand. For another, I've long been haunted by the fear of hitting the batter.

I still turn sick when I recall the picture of Hank Lieber, the New York Giants' outfielder, sprawled beside home plate after one of my curves hit him in the head in the spring of 1937. Some pitchers will tell you that the intentional "duster" is a legitimate weapon.

It is one I never used.

But there's a difference between anger and resentment, and I must confess that I was resentful when I started against the New York Yankees in their own Stadium the afternoon of

April 30, 1946. Whether or not my attitude affected my pitching is a question which no one can answer. In any case, the game turned out to be the one I call the greatest of my career. When it was over, I had my second no-hitter.

The resentment which I mention was not directed against the Yankees. On the contrary, I had at least as many good friends on that fine New York team as on any of the Indian's other rivals. The Yankees just happened to furnish the opposition on a day when I wanted desperately to prove something.

I suppose the story really opens in the training season. It was to be my first full year after the war. I felt that I was far from the twilight of my career, but it was a fact that from my kid days at home in Iowa, and through six prewar years with the Indians, I had thrown a great number of baseballs at a high rate of speed. At the age of twenty-seven, I couldn't see much point in calling on the full resources of my arm on every pitch. I no longer was anxious to strike out every exhibition game opponent who stepped to the plate.

As a result, my barnstorming performances were not exactly magnificent. I was confident that I'd be ready when the bell rang, but this opinion was not shared unanimously by the reporters who watched me work. From time to time, a critic made tentative motions in the direction of a guess that I no longer could win consistently.

Such comment didn't worry me, and when I shut out the Chicago White Sox, on opening day, 1 to 0—with the help of a miracle catch by Bob Lemon, then playing center field—I felt that my conditioning methods had been justified.

But Virgin Trucks and his fellow Tigers beat me in my next start, 3 to 2, and Joe Haynes of the White Sox shut us out, 4 to 0, the next time my turn rolled around. That did it, at least for one wire service writer. The readers of hundreds of newspapers from coast to coast were told by implication if not by direct statement that they could drop the name of Feller from the list of front-rank pitchers.

I thought that the story was not only premature. I considered it unfair. I was thoroughly angry when I read the piece, but by the time we reached New York on our first eastern trip, my feeling had congealed into an icy determination to let my arm deliver my rebuttal.

I wanted to pitch a great game that afternoon of April 30. Of course, I wasn't even dreaming of a no-hitter. No pitcher does—especially when the opposing line-up is composed of such hitters as Joe DiMaggio, Bill Dickey, Joe Gordon, Charley Keller, Tommy Henrich, George Stirnweiss, Nick Etten and Phil Rizzuto.

Floyd Bevens was chosen to pitch for the Yankees and the game got under way on schedule. Rizzuto bounced out to Ken Keltner to open the home half of the first. Stirnweiss grounded sharply to my left and the ball skidded off the side of the mound and squirmed toward the right of second base. Lou Boudreau, who had started from deep short, somehow got to that ball, cutting across behind the mound and scooping up the grounder between hops. He was traveling so fast that he turned a somersault as he threw to Les Fleming at first base for the put-out. I've seen Boudreau make many an "impossible" play, but that one stands out in my memory as his best. I thought so even at the time. I didn't know then, of course, that it was the play which would enable me to write a bit of baseball history.

For that was the closest the Yankees came to a base hit in those nine rugged innings. They collected five bases on balls and one player reached base on an error. Eleven of them were strikeout victims.

In each of the first four innings, I had a man on base by the free ticket route. In the fifth, I finally set the Yankees down in order, with Gordon flying out and Dickey and Bevens fanning. Rizzuto walked to open the sixth and Stirnweiss bunted him to second, but Henrich fouled out and DiMaggio flied out.

In the seventh, Keller, Etten and Gordon were retired in order. As I walked to the dugout, I could hear the expectant hum in the stands. There were 37,144 fans out that day. Not only did they know that I had at least an outside chance to finish with a no-hit game, but they realized they were watching an exceptional pitchers' battle. We had made a few hits off Bevens, but not a single run.

We remained scoreless in our half of the eighth. Once more I nailed the Yanks in order in their half, with Boudreau again contributing handsomely when he threw out the fleet Rizzuto from deep short.

In the top of the ninth, Frank Hayes, our catcher that day, pulled one of Bevens' pitches into the left field stands for the only run of the afternoon. We were leading now, and only

the last of the ninth stood between me and my second trip
to the Hall of Fame.

Only the last of the ninth. Only Stirnweiss, Henrich and
DiMaggio, with Keller following if one of them reached base.
I looked around at our infielders before I took my wind-up.
They were grim and pale with tension. I suddenly was glad
that all I had to do was pitch.

Stirnweiss hit a bounder down the first base line, but Fleming tried to start for first before he had a good grip on the
ball. He fumbled for an error. Playing to get back that one
big run, Henrich sacrificed. Stirnweiss was on second, with
DiMaggio swinging calmly as he waited for me to return to
the rubber. I don't know how long I pitched to DiMaggio.
It seemed to be hours. He fouled off pitch after pitch. The
count went to three and two. Then he grounded hard to
Boudreau, who retired him as Stirnweiss moved to third.

THE BOX SCORE
(*April 30, 1946*)

CLEVELAND	A.B.	R.	H.	P.	A.	NEW YORK (A)	A.B.	R.	H.	P.	A.
Case, lf.	4	0	2	1	0	Rizzuto, ss.	3	0	0	5	5
Lemon, cf.	4	0	1	1	0	Stirnweiss, 3b.	3	0	0	1	2
Edwards, rf.	2	0	0	0	0	Henrich, rf.	1	0	0	0	0
Fleming, 1b.	3	0	1	9	0	DiMaggio, cf.	4	0	0	1	0
Keltner, 3b.	1	0	0	0	3	Keller, lf.	3	0	0	3	0
Boudreau, ss.	3	0	0	0	4	Etten, 1b.	3	0	0	8	0
Hayes, c.	4	1	2	12	1	Gordon, 2b.	3	0	0	3	3
Mack, 2b.	3	0	1	4	3	Dickey, c.	2	0	0	6	3
Feller, p.	4	0	0	0	1	Bevens, p.	3	0	0	0	2
Totals	28	1	7	27	12	Totals	25	0	0	27	15

CLEVELAND	0	0	0	0	0	0	0	0	1—1
NEW YORK (A)	0	0	0	0	0	0	0	0	0—0

Errors—Fleming, Keltner, Rizzuto, Bevens. Run batted in—Hayes.
Home run—Hayes. Stolen bases—Case, Henrich. Sacrifices—Boudreau,
Keltner, Stirnweiss, Edwards, Henrich. Double plays—Gordon, Rizzuto
and Etten; Stirnweiss, Rizzuto and Etten; Dickey and Rizzuto. Left on
base—Cleveland 8, New York 5. Bases on balls—Bevens 5, Feller 5.
Strikeouts—Bevens 5, Feller 11. Umpires—Rommel, Boyer and Jones.
Time—2:14. Attendance—38,112.

I forgot about Stirnweiss. He wasn't likely to attempt to
steal home, with Keller at the plate. Charley didn't put me
through the wringer as DiMaggio had done. To this day, I

can't tell you which pitch he hit, but it was an early one—
and the ball bounced toward big Ray Mack, our second baseman, the same fine infielder who had made the last assist of
my first no-hitter six years earlier.

Ray charged the ball and fell to his knees. That could have
meant disaster, for the official scorer hardly could have
charged him with an error if he had failed to complete the
play. But he was up in time to make the stop. Never on any
baseball field have I heard a sound so sweet as the thump of
his throw in Fleming's glove.

JIMMY FOXX

as told to Lyall Smith

Only Ruth before him has hit more home runs than James Emory Foxx. His total of 534 was accumulated over a period of 20 years, and his long distance clouting helped the Philadelphia Athletics to their pennants of 1929, 1930 and 1931. After 11 years with the A's, Jimmy spent seven with the Red Sox before closing out his career in the National League. Born October 22, 1907, in Sudlersville, Maryland, Mr. Double X managed in the minors before retiring from the game.

He was hired by several ball clubs to help young hitters in spring training. He died, at 59, on July 21, 1967, in Miami, Florida. He lived long enough to see Willie Mays break his career home run record and become second to Ruth.

I GUESS I've hit just about as many home runs as anyone still wearing a baseball uniform but for just one good solid punch I'd have to take the afternoon in the fifth game of the 1930 World Series when I smacked one into the stands as a personal tribute to Mr. Mack (Manager Connie Mack of the A's).

But there were other afternoons, too, that I'll never forget. Some were before that day in '30, some after but most were wound up in one way or another with Mr. Mack.

I met him the first year I ever played. That was in 1925 when the A's bought me as a kid of 17 with nothing but a bunch of muscles and a big desperate lunge at the ball.

That previous fall I'd received one of those penny post cards from Frank "Home Run" Baker who was managing a team in the Eastern League and that was a thrill, too. I was just 16 when I got this card. Baker had scribbled on the back: "Would you be interested in being a professional ballplayer? If you are contact me." Naturally I wrote him and he signed me up. That next summer he sold me to the Athletics who shipped me out for seasoning.

I was hitting pretty good then and kept right on till the A's brought me up again to help out Cy Perkins, one of the best catchers I ever saw. I didn't have much to do until 1927 when Mr. Mack stuck me over at third base. I played there a while and then Ossie Orwoll, our first baseman, got into a slump and one day after I had been warming up a pitcher in the bullpen Mr. Mack walked over to me.

"Ever play first base, Jimmy?" he asked. I told him no. "You are today," he said, and tossed me a first baseman's mitt.

That '29 season was a big one for me. I was still pretty young but I didn't have to do very much on a team that was as murderous as any I ever saw.

We had Bishop and Haas, Cochrane and Simmons, Miller and Dykes, and pitchers like Earnshaw, Ehmke, Walberg, Grove and Quinn. That was the year we breezed to an American League pennant and faced the Cubs in the Series.

In the first game I smacked a homer off Charlie Root to break a scoreless tie in the 7th inning and help us win 3–1. I hit another one in the second game when we slapped them around 9–3 and had a lot of fun in the fourth game when we made those 10 runs in the 7th inning after trailing 8–0. I didn't hit any long ones in that game but poked out a couple of singles to take part in the big spree.

But that was nothing like the buzz I got the next year when we went into the Series again. The Cards had won the National title and were giving us a stiff battle. In that first game we were up against Burleigh Grimes and his spitter. He was tough to hit when he gave that ball a working-over and was really putting the stuff on it that day.

In the second inning I came up after Al Simmons had bounced out to Grimes and I stepped in to one of Burleigh's spitters and slapped it off the right field wall over Ray Blades' head for a triple. Bing Miller was up next. He hit a long fly that time out to Blades again and I came in with the first run after the catch.

I felt pretty good about that but old Burleigh wasn't through with me yet. In the fourth I was up again right after Simmons had poked out a home run to tie the score, but Burleigh fooled me on a low spitter and I struck out. In the sixth we went ahead when Maxie Bishop worked Grimes for a walk and scored when Jimmy Dykes doubled. With two out Burleigh walked Simmons on purpose to get at me.

I fell right into his plans and was easy for him. I was expecting him to throw me a spitter if the count was close. And it was for I worked him up to a 3–2 with two runners on base and two out.

Burleigh stood out there and went through his motions. He put the glove up to his mouth, looked out at Dykes on second, glanced over at Simmons on first. Then stepped off the mound and turned around for another look at the scoreboard. Then he took his stance again and pitched. I was sure it'd be a spitter, a low one around the knees like the one he had fanned me on in the second inning. But it was a curve, a fast hopper that came in waist high and caught me way off balance.

Everybody was surprised for Burleigh didn't throw a curve very often. But they weren't nearly as surprised as I was. I stood there at the plate for a minute still trying to figure out what had happened, but I was out.

We won that game anyway and took the second one before moving down to St. Louis feeling pretty good. Then Wild Bill Hallahan shut us out 5–0 before Jess Haines set us down on four hits to beat Lefty Grove 3–1 and even up the Series at two games apiece.

Well, we're in St. Louis for the fifth game and all of us are keyed up pretty high. We wanted to win that one, for any baseball man will tell you that the fifth game is the big one. If you win it you're over the hump and coasting. If you lose it—well, that's not good at all.

It's Grimes' turn again and Mr. Mack picks out big George Earnshaw to go for us. Mr. Mack took me to one side of the dugout just before the game started. "Jimmy," he said, "you watch out for that pitcher out there. He figures he has your number and I think he'll try to get to you if he gets in a pinch. And watch for that curve ball. Don't let him fool you with that spitter motion. Just because he goes through like he's going to throw it is no sign he will."

The game starts and right away you can tell it's going to be a honey. Both Grimes and Earnshaw are really tough, although Mike Cochrane gets a single for us in the first inning and Adams pokes one off Ehmke.

I come up in the second and hit the first pitch, a fast ball, out to Chick Hafey in deep left for just another out and then come up again in the fifth. I swing on the first pitch again and poke a single into center field for our second single and the third hit of the game, but it doesn't do any good and nobody scores.

I bat again in the seventh and Burleigh gets me in a 2—1 hole. I'm still thinking about a curve ball when he throws a fast one past me and all I hit was a big hunk of air.

They scared us in their half when Jimmy Wilson doubled

THE BOX SCORE
(October 6, 1930)

ATHLETICS	A.B.	R.	H.	P.	A.	CARDINALS	A.B.	R.	H.	P.	A.
Bishop, 2b.	4	0	0	1	0	Douthit, cf.	4	0	0	2	0
Dykes, 3b.	3	0	0	0	1	Adams, 3b.	4	0	1	0	1
Cochrane, c.	3	1	1	7	1	Frisch, 2b.	4	0	1	3	3
Simmons, lf.	4	0	0	3	0	Bottomley, 1b.	4	0	0	9	1
Foxx, 1b.	4	1	2	12	0	Hafey, lf.	3	0	0	1	0
Miller, rf.	4	0	0	0	0	Watkins, rf.	3	0	0	1	0
Haas, cf.	4	0	1	2	0	Wilson, c.	4	0	1	9	0
Boley, ss.	3	0	1	2	1	Gelbert, ss.	2	0	0	2	8
Earnshaw, p.	2	0	0	0	4	Grimes, p.	2	0	0	0	0
Moore	0	0	0	0	0	Blades	0	0	0	0	0
Grove, p.	0	0	0	0	1						
Totals	31	2	5	27	8	Totals	30	0	3	27	13

Moore batted for Earnshaw in 8th.

Blades batted for Watkins in 9th.

ATHLETICS	0	0	0	0	0	0	0	0	0	2—2
CARDINALS	0	0	0	0	0	0	0	0	0	0—0

Error—Frisch. Home run—Foxx. Sacrifice hit—Grimes. Double play—Adams to Frisch to Bottomley. Left on bases—St. Louis 8, Philadelphia 5. Bases on balls—Off Grimes 3 (Dykes, Moore, Cochrane); off Earnshaw 3 (Gelbert 2, Hafey); off Grove 1 (Blades). Struck out—By Grimes 7 (Bishop 2, Boley, Cochrane, Earnshaw, Foxx, Miller); by Earnshaw 5 (Watkins, Bottomley 2, Adams, Hafey); by Grove 2 (Bottomley, Gelbert). Hits—Off Earnshaw 2 in 7 innings, off Grove 1 in 2 innings. Winning pitcher—Grove. Umpires—Moriarty, plate; Rigler, first; Geisel, second; Reardon, third. Time—1:53.

down the line, but there were two outs and Mr. Mack waved his score card for George to walk Gelbert to get at Grimes. Burleigh hit one hard, but Mule Haas ran it down and we were out of the jam.

In the eighth we had a good chance to score when two singles and an error by Frankie Frisch loaded the bases with only one out. But Burleigh reached down into his bag of tricks to make Bishop ground to Bottomley, who forced Haas at the plate, and make Dykes hit one to Gelbert at short, who flipped to Frisch in time to force Bishop to end the inning.

Earnshaw had been lifted for a pinch hitter in that frame and Mr. Mack put in Lefty Grove, who got by the Card half, although he was nicked for a single, the third Redbird hit, by Frisch.

Then came the ninth. There still was no score. Each team had made only three hits and Grimes was bearing down. But he pitched too carefully to Cochrane and Mickey jogged down to first base on a pass. Al Simmons came up, but he undercut a spitter and lifted a high pop fly to Gelbert for the first out. That brought me up again.

I was nervous. But Grimes was cool as ice. He was deliberately slow in getting ready to pitch, so I stepped out of the box. I got some dirt on my hands and stepped in again. He raised his hand to his mouth in his spitter motion. Then he threw the first pitch. I knew in that flash second it wasn't a spitter, for it was coming in close. It was a curve and I swung!

Well, that was it. The big thrill. I heard the Athletic bench yell all at once and there it went. Some fan reached up and pulled it down when it hit in the left-field bleachers for a home run.

FRANKIE F. FRISCH

as told to Ken Smith

Frankie F. Frisch, Jr., born September 9, 1898, in New York City, came off Fordham University's campus some twenty-one years later to spark John McGraw's New York Giant infield of the early '20s. Frisch was traded to the St. Louis Cardinals, and started to lose his hair when he became manager of the rambunctious Gas House Gang in 1933. Frisch took over the managership at Pittsburgh, later broadcasting ball games before he managed the Cubs. He is a member of the Hall of Fame.

Now nearly 70, Frisch diligently tends his flower garden at his house in Bradford, Rhode Island, and tells anyone who'll listen how sissified baseball has become compared with his Gas House Gang days.

I FINALLY got to sleep on the night of October 8, 1934, in my hotel in Detroit. The next day was the most important day of my whole baseball career so far, and I knew it.

When I had been a fresh kid, with John J. McGraw's Giants in the 1921, '22, '23 and '24 World Series, I never fretted about anything. Slept like a baby and played with an abandon I wish I had had in the three Series during the '30s. McGraw and the older men like Dave Bancroft, Heinie Groh and Casey Stengel did the worrying in the old days. A young squirt isn't afraid of anything.

But in the 1930, '31 and '34 Series, the responsibility was terrific. This stuff you hear about old codgers mellowing and losing the competitive urge is the bunk. It grows stronger with age, especially when you are playing second base and managing the Gas House Gang.

Well, we were even-Stephen at three games apiece, in the 1934 Series—the Cardinals against the Tigers. You can imagine how I would feel if we blew this, of all Series, after such a Donnybrook as we had been through. I lay there in the sheets, figuring pitches for Mickey Cochrane, Charley Gehringer, Goose Goslin and Hank Greenberg, knowing that here was the one big game of my life whether I played a personal part in the playing end, or not, I don't have to thumb back and say: "Let's see, now, which WAS my biggest day?"

You can imagine what was on my mind lying there before the seventh and deciding game. Dizzy Dean had won the first for us in Detroit, 8–3. Schoolboy Rowe, who had a tremendous year with the Tigers, had beaten us the second game, 3–2, the Schoolboy retiring 22 batters in a row starting with the fourth inning. Paul Dean had won the third battle, but the Tigers had taken the fourth and fifth, and the city of Detroit was beginning to lay the red carpet.

Then Paul came back and won the sixth game with a single, 4–3, I'll never forget old Dizzy hugging Paul in the dressing room after the game, wrestling him and yelping, "You're the greatest pitcher the Dean family ever had," and then Diz would pound everybody else on the back and brag about his kid brother. Diz had announced at the start of the year "me and Paul will win 50 games," and they'd darn near done it, Dean winning 30 and Paul 19. Diz had said they'd murder the Tigers in the Series, too, and now they had between them won three games—the only ones we had taken.

I remember John Carmichael coming up to me in the confusion of that dressing room after the sixth game and asking, "Dean tomorrow—the other Dean?" and me sitting there, all in from the strain, and answering, "If I last till tomorrow."

Carmichael took one look at Diz charging around the room with a white pith helmet and hollering how he'd take the seventh game tomorrow. Carmichael said, "Wild horses can't keep Dean off that mound tomorrow, Frank."

I looked. Dizzy had a rubber tiger, a Detroit souvenir, by the tail and was whacking Bill DeLancey over the head with it and then throwing it into the showers at Pepper Martin. I knew inside me Diz would pitch it. He had a terrible head cold and only two days before had been knocked out running the bases, but there'd be no use fighting against it—he was the boy and the chips were sure down.

Incidentally the wolves had been on me for putting in Dizzy to run for big, slow Virgil Davis in that fourth game—the time Diz went into second so high and hard that Charley Gehringer, trying for a forceout, hit Diz in the head. But I didn't mind the criticism. We were out to win. We were the Gas House Gang and I knew Diz would give 'em something to worry about running bases as well as pitching.

Well, morning came for the big game and then at the park Diz took the ball and warmed up with what looked like 50,000 Tiger fans hooting at him, and him grinning and yelling at each of us, "I'll shut 'em out. Get me a couple of runs: that's all. I'll blank the blank-blank blankety-blanks."

Dizzy said he'd shut 'em out and he did. And with the score 0–0 to start the third he singled and stretched it to get to second.

Pepper Martin, the Wild Horse, was up next and he hit a slow hopper to Greenberg and went down so fast he beat the throw. Three years before Pepper had driven Mickey Cochrane crazy running bases in the Series between the Athletics and the Cards and now he did it again.

Then Auker walked Rothrock and the bases were full. And I was up. I couldn't let the rest of them make an old man out of the playing-manager, so I doubled and all three of 'em came in.

That was all for Auker and in came Schoolboy Rowe. Our bench stood up and gave him the "How'm-I-doin'-Edna?" chant. He had asked that during a radio interview, throwing in a little message to his girl, and the papers had been riding him about it. Rip Collins welcomed Rowe with a double and I scored—and away went Schoolboy.

We kept on hitting, and Cochrane, who was fit to be asylumed by this time, kept bringing in more pitchers. Dizzy got his second hit of the inning by racing like Pepper to first on a slow grounder, bringing DeLancey in. By the time the inning was over we had seven runs and I figured maybe Dizzy would be winded by all that hitting and base running he'd done in the inning, but, heck, no. He beat the rest of the team out to position and could hardly take time to make his warmup throws.

It was like playing ball at the foot of Vesuvius. And in

the sixth came the eruption. Pepper started by singling and, seeing Goslin in left juggle the throw momentarily, he went on to second. Rothrock and I went out, but Medwick lammed the ball against the screen for a double and kept on to third, sliding in hard. Marv Owen on third got the ball and stepped on Medwick's leg. Joe kicked up from his position on his back and hit Owen in the chest. They started to

THE BOX SCORE
(October 9, 1934)

St. Louis	A.B.	R.	H.	P.	A.	Detroit	A.B.	R.	H.	P.	A.
Martin, 3b.	5	3	2	0	1	White, cf.	4	0	0	3	0
Rothrock, rf.	5	1	2	4	0	Cochrane, c.	4	0	0	2	2
Frisch, 2b.	5	1	1	3	5	Hayworth, c.	0	0	0	1	0
Medwick, lf.	4	1	1	1	0	Gehringer, 2b.	4	0	2	3	5
Fullis, lf.	1	0	1	1	0	Goslin, lf.	4	0	0	4	0
Collins, 1b.	5	1	4	7	2	Rogell, ss.	4	0	1	3	2
DeLancey, c.	5	1	1	5	0	Greenberg, 1b.	4	0	1	7	0
Orsatti, cf.	3	1	1	2	0	Owen, 3b.	4	0	0	1	2
Durocher, ss.	5	1	2	3	4	Fox, rf.	3	0	2	3	0
J. Dean, p.	5	1	2	1	0	Auker, p.	0	0	0	0	0
						Rowe, p.	0	0	0	0	0
						Hogsett, p.	0	0	0	0	0
						Bridges, p.	2	0	0	0	1
						Marberry, p.	0	0	0	0	0
						G. Walker	1	0	0	0	0
						Crowder, p.	0	0	0	0	0
Totals	43	11	17	27	12	Totals	34	0	6	27	12

G. Walker batted for Marberry in 8th.

St. Louis	0	0	7	0	0	2	2	0	0—11
Detroit	0	0	0	0	0	0	0	0	0— 0

Errors—Collins, White, Gehringer, Goslin. Two-base hits—Rothrock (2), Fox (2), Frisch, DeLancey. Three-base hits—Medwick, Durocher. Runs batted in—Frisch (3), Collins (2), Martin, Rothrock, Medwick, J. Dean, DeLancey. Stolen base—Martin. Double play—Owen, Gehringer, Greenberg. Bases on balls—Off Auker 1 (Rothrock), off Hogsett 2 (Orsatti, Martin), off Marberry 1 (Orsatti). Struck out—By Auker 1 (Martin), by Bridges 2 (J. Dean, DeLancey), by Crowder 1 (Rothrock), by J. Dean 5 (Greenberg (3), Bridges, White). Pitching records —Auker 6 hits, 4 runs in 2 1-3 innings; Rowe 2 hits in 1-3 inning; Hogsett 2 hits, 1 run in 0 inning (pitched to 4 batters); Bridges 6 hits, 4 runs in 4 1-3 innings, Marberry 1 hit, 0 runs in 1 inning; Crowder 0 hits, 0 runs in 1 inning. Left on bases—St. Louis 9, Detroit 7. Earned runs—St. Louis 10, Detroit 0. Caught stealing—Orsatti. Losing pitcher —Auker. Umpires—Geisel (A.L.) home plate; Reardon (N.L.) first base; Klem (N.L.) third base. Time of game—2:19.

fight, and both teams boiled out. The panic was on, but nothing to what happened after the umpires had quieted everybody down and got the inning played out. As Medwick went out to left field the Tiger fans met him with cushions, bottles, lemons, and some of them took off their shoes and tried to bean him. They tried to climb the 18-foot wire fence to murder him. For 15 minutes the game was stopped and finally Commissioner Landis told Cochrane and me to bring Owen and Medwick up to his box. He asked Medwick, "Did you kick him?" and Joe said "You're darn right, I did!" They wouldn't shake hands and the noise got worse. Cochrane would run out and beg the bleachers to be good, but they would have none of his advice. So Landis put both Medwick and Owen out of the game and we went on to finish it.

So it ended 11–0. Dizzy had done what he said he'd do and we'd done more than he asked us.

BOB GIBSON

as told by Jack Orr

Robert Gibson, born in Omaha, Nebraska, November 9, 1935, hadn't much good fortune as a boy. His father died three months before Bob was born; his mother worked in a laundry to support her seven children. Gibson was so sickly that his mother "never thought he'd pull through." He had rickets, hay fever, asthma, pneumonia and a rheumatic heart. Yet when he grew up he worked his way through Creighton University, played basketball and baseball there, spent a year with the famed Harlem Globetrotters and signed with the St. Louis Cardinals when he was 21. He became one of the fiercest, hardest-throwing pitchers in the game. When his baseball days are ended, Gibson wants to be a youth counselor.

THE MOST dramatic confrontation of the 1967 World Series was the seventh and final game which saw the Cardinals' Bob Gibson face the astonishing Red Sox' Jim Lonborg. Each had pitched two brilliant games earlier in the Series. Each was the ace of his team's staff. Each had a history of gritty determination that set them apart from their fellow professionals.

As it turned out, the game wasn't much of a contest. Gibson, working smoothly and almost automatically, subdued the Red Sox on three hits, smashed a homer in his own behalf and brought the world championship to St. Louis with a convincing 7–2 victory before 35,188 almost-silent Boston fans. Gibson was so good that he left those rooting for the underdog Red Sox with a sense of futility which grew as the innings rolled on.

Gibson was named the outstanding player of the Series almost mechanically, though he himself demurred ("I think they should have named Lou Brock," referring to his remarkable teammate who hit .414), most fans believed Gibson's achievements worthy of any honor you could name.

For his victory that day put his name into juxtaposition with some of the game's legendary figures and provided material for future stars to shoot at. Some of his achievements:

By pitching five complete-game victories in succession— he won his last two starts against the New York Yankees in the 1964 World Series—he matched a feat accomplished only by Red Ruffing of the Yankees over four different Series, in 1937, 1938, 1939 and 1941. By allowing only 14 hits in his three games, Gibson matched Christy Mathewson's figure for least hits allowed in three completed Series games. By starting, finishing and winning three games in one Series, Gibson joined select company. Only Mathewson, Babe Adams of Pittsburgh in 1909, Jack Combs of the Athletics in 1910, Stanley Covaleski of Cleveland in 1920 and Lew Burdette of Milwaukee in 1957 had done it before.

The magnificence of Bob's performance was belittled by the pitcher himself. He is a reticent subject for interviews, even though he conducts a radio-television program in Omaha. But pressed by newsmen and broadcasters, he admitted that his performance in the seventh game was the greatest day of his career. He relied on his 90-mile-an-hour fast ball for the most part, even in the late innings when the heavy work load he had endured began telling on his arm.

"He is just too much," said Tim McCarver, the Cardinal catcher. "He goes by sheer guts. When things get tough, he just gets tougher." (That comment had a familiar ring. In 1964, after Gibson had beaten the Yankees in the seventh game of the World Series, his then manager, Johnny Keane, had observed: "He pitched the last three innings on sheer guts, just throwing the fast ball. I've never had a gutsier player." On that occasion the Yankees had pulled the game close on a homer by Mickey Mantle in the sixth inning. Keane went out to talk to Gibson and reported later. "I was thinking possibly of taking him out," Keane said, "but then I looked at his face, so determined looking, and that reassured me. He had a look which told me automatically that he'd be all right." And he was.)

Gibson's performance in 1967 was even more remarkable when his injury is taken into consideration. His right leg was fractured in mid-July by a line drive off the bat of Roberto Clemente of the Pirates and he was out of action for eight weeks. But he bounced back to pitch four games in regular season play in September and registered three classic performances in the Series. Big Bob (he stands six-one and weighs close to 200 pounds) won the first game on a six-hitter, 2–1; took the fourth game on a five-hitter, 6–0; and breezed through the finale with a three-hit notch on his glove.

He had had other misfortunes earlier in his career. In 1962, though he won 15 games, he suffered a broken ankle while taking batting practice. A recurrence of an asthma attack slowed him in 1963, but he still won 18, and in 1964 his arm went lame for an 18-day stretch limiting his victory total to 19. In 1966 a nerve injury in his right elbow kept him from the All-Star game.

On the day of the big game in 1967, Cardinal manager Red Schoendienst quietly wrote out his starting lineup, after conferring with his old roommate, Stan Musial, general manager. Then Schoendienst for the first time in the Series decided to forgo a team meeting. Asked why, Red smiled, shrugged and said, "I have Gibson. I just give the ball to Gibson and get out of the way."

Gibson later admitted that he grew tired in this most critical of games. He said that he felt the fatigue from the sixth inning on, though holding a 7–1 lead. He said that he had dismissed the idea of pitching a no-hit game, because "I am a high fast-ball pitcher, and that type doesn't usually get no-hitters."

Still the question was raised as to whether Gibson would finish without help. He had struck out eight hitters in the first five innings, and had recorded an important out in the first inning when he made Carl Yastrzemski, the Sox most feared slugger, pop up after an opening walk to Joey Foy and a sacrifice. Gibson didn't walk another man until Yastrzemski led off the seventh, but nothing developed.

Rico Petrocelli opened the eighth with a double into the left field corner, the second Red Sox hit, and took third

THE BOX SCORE
(October 12, 1967)

St. Louis	A.B.	R.	H.	P.	A.	Boston	A.B.	R.	H.	P.	A.
Brock, lf.	4	1	2	1	0	Foy, 3b.	3	0	0	2	3
Flood, cf.	3	1	1	0	0	Morehead, p.	0	0	0	0	0
Maris, rf.	3	0	2	1	0	Osinski, p.	0	0	0	0	0
Cepeda, 1b.	5	0	0	6	2	Brett, p.	0	0	0	0	0
McCarver, c.	5	1	1	12	0	Andrews, 2b.	3	0	0	1	2
Shannon, 3b.	4	1	0	0	0	Yastrze'ski, lf.	3	0	1	2	0
Javier, 2b.	4	1	2	4	4	Harrelson, rf.	4	0	0	3	0
Maxvill, ss.	4	1	1	3	3	Scott, 1b.	4	1	1	9	0
B. Gibson, p.	4	1	1	0	1	Smith, cf.	3	0	0	2	0
						Petrocelli, ss.	3	1	1	3	2
						Howard, c.	2	0	0	4	1
						bJones, 3b.	0	0	0	0	0
						Lonborg, p.	1	0	0	0	0
						aTartabull	1	0	0	0	0
						Santiago, p.	0	0	0	0	0
						cSiebern	1	0	0	0	0
						R. Gibson, c.	0	0	0	1	0
Totals	36	7	10	27	10	Totals	28	2	3	27	8

```
St. Louis    0 0 2  0 2 3  0 0 0—7
Boston       0 0 0  0 1 0  0 1 0—2
```

St. Louis	IP.	H.	R.	ER.	Boston	IP.	H.	R.	ER.
B. Gibson (Winner)	9	3	2	2	Lonborg (Loser)	6	10	7	6
					Santiago	2	0	0	0
					Morehead	⅓	0	0	0
					Osinski	⅓	0	0	0
					Brett	⅓	0	0	0

Bases on balls—Off B. Gibson 3 (Foy, Yastrzemski, Jones), off Lonborg 1 (Flood), off Morehead 3 (Brock, Flood, Maris). Struck out—By B. Gibson 10 (Harrelson 2, Scott 2, Petrocelli 2, Lonborg, Foy, Andrews, Tartabull), by Lonborg 3 (Javier, Shannon, Flood), by Santiago 1 (Cepeda), by Morehead 1 (B. Gibson).

aStruck out for Longborg in sixth. bWalked for Howard in eighth. cHit into force play for Santiago in eighth. Runs batted in—Flood, Maris, Javier 3, B. Gibson, Siebern. Two-base hits—McCarver, Brock, Petrocelli. Three-base hits—Maxvill, Scott. Home runs—B. Gibson, Javier. Stolen bases—Brock 3. Sacrifice hit—Andrews. Sacrifice fly—Maris. Double play—Maxvill, Javier and Cepeda. Wild pitches—Lonborg, B. Gibson. Left on bases—St. Louis 7, Boston 3. Umpires—Stevens (AL) plate, Barlick (NL) first base, Umont (AL) second base, Donatelli (NL) third base, Runge (AL) left field, Pryor (NL) right field. Time—2.23. Attendance—35,188.

on a wild pitch. Dalton Jones, a pinch-hitter, walked, but Norm Siebern, another pinch-swinger, forced Jones as the second Boston run came in, and two more grounders ended the inning.

Now it was the eighth inning and Yastrzemski opened the inning with a single. "I thought he might be getting into trouble," Schoendienst said later, "so I went out to the mound. 'Look,' I said, 'you've got a five-run lead. Just get the ball over and make them hit it.' " Gibson responded by making Ken Harrelson rap into a double play and he fanned the strong George Scott to end the Series and the baseball season.

In the celebration that followed in the Cardinal clubhouse, almost all of the Cardinals horsed around pouring champagne, shaving lather and beer on each other. One of the quiet ones was Gibson who said with some embarrassment that his hometown, Omaha, was going to give him a parade, even to the extent of letting the schoolchildren off for the day. "No, I'm not making any speeches. I'll just wave," he said. In another corner, another Cardinal hero, Roger Maris, was commenting, "I'm certainly glad I'm playing with him instead of against him. He's a tiger out there. And you know if you get him a run or two, he'll win it for you."

Since Gibson was only 31 when he pitched his masterpiece, and since the Cardinals have an impressive young lineup to go with him, it is likely he will add to his already existing marks in the years ahead.

But for that one day in Fenway Park in 1967, chalk it up as Gibson's greatest.

LEFTY GOMEZ

as told to John Drohan

Vernon Louis "Goofy" Gomez was born November 26, 1910, in Rodeo, California. He came to the New York Yankees in 1930 with an undernourished body, spontaneity of youth and reckless abandon. He clowned his way through the next 12 seasons, but never neglected his trade—pitching winning baseball with a blazing fast ball. After hanging up six World Series triumphs without a loss, three All-Star game victories and a tentful of laughs, all with the Yankees, Lefty closed out his career as a member of the Boston Braves in 1943.

Now a sporting goods salesman, the witty Gomez is a familiar figure at spring training bases and at ball parks throughout the year.

To TELL the truth, in relating my biggest baseball day, I'm torn between two loves. I'm something like the Old Soak who never knew whether his wife told him to take one drink and come home at 12, or take 12 and come home at 1. Of course, there have been complaints. I've been a pitcher. On the other hand, there was a hot day one August in Washington—and can it get hot there—when I got four for five, as they say down at the clubhouse.

I'd like to dwell a bit on that, because those days have been rare in my career. But inasmuch as I've drawn my best salary checks for pitching, rather than hitting, I'll pass it up, much as I dislike to. However, the fact I got four for five might have had something to do with Bucky Harris resigning his job a few weeks later.

Searching the old cerebellum, I think my biggest thrill in baseball was my first World Series game. It was against the Chicago Cubs in the second game of the 1932 Series.

Red Ruffing had won the first game, 12–6 from Guy Bush at the Yankee Stadium and I was to work the second against Lon Warneke, the Arkansas Humming Bird.

Joe McCarthy had us hopped up to pour it on the Cubs and lick 'em quick. He'd got the old heave-ho from the Cubs only two years before, and was anxious to get back at them. He figured he hadn't got such a good shake in Chicago and often said he'd like to get even. This was his chance.

Revenge couldn't be as sweet to him as if Rogers Hornsby had stayed as manager of the Cubs. Hornsby had succeeded McCarthy as manager of the Cubs in 1931 and then had been given the old heave-ho in his turn in August, '32. That had brought in Charley Grimm as Cub manager, and the club has turned it on hot to come down the stretch whooping and hollering and wicking everybody out of their way to grab the flag in one of baseball's best stretch drives.

The Yanks under Huggins had swept the World Series four straight from the Pirates in '27 and again from the Cards in '28, and McCarthy naturally wanted to do what Miller had done. We figured we could do it, for while Grimm had Jurges, Herman, Koenig and English with him on the infield, Cuyler, Stephenson and Demaree in the outfield, Hartnett catching and Warneke, Root, Malone, Bush, Grimes and Jakie May pitching, we had what we thought was a much stronger club, with Dickey catching, Gehrig on first, Crosetti at short, Lazzeri at second, Sewell at third, Babe Ruth, Sam Chapman and Earle Combs in the outfield and Red Ruffing, Wilcy Moore, Johnny Allen, George Pipgras and myself.

There was a lot of talk, as the second game came up, about the kid-competition between Lon Warneke and me—two bean poles. Both of us were sophomores; he was 23, I was 21; he had won 22 that summer for the Cubs, I had managed to get by with 24 for the Yanks.

Babe Ruth was 37 and beginning to slow down in the field, but he could still flatten the ball and had hit 41 homers that year.

I remember how Ed Barrow, our general manager, kept after me all my first and second years to put on weight. It scared him when he looked at me, for I weighed only 152, which was thin enough for my height, over 6 feet. Barrow figured I couldn't last.

At the end of the first season he told me, "About 25 years ago we had a pitcher around here named Jack Chesbro, the first pitcher ever to win 16 straight games in the American League. If you'd only put on more weight you could make the fans forget Chesbro."

I wasn't any fatter my second year, '32, but I could fire the ball through a two-inch plank. Barrow, however, kept after me, and I knew during the series that I'd have to spend the winter at a health resort in California Barrow had picked out—a sort of old ladies' home were I was to fatten up.

Incidentally, I did come back to start the '33 season 20 pounds fatter and they put me to rooming with Pat Malone, whom McCarthy had bought from the Cubs, who was a fat man.

That '33 season y won only 16 and lost 10 and instead of making the fans forget Chesbro I was making 'em forget Gomez, so that winter of '33–35 I took off so much weight I showed up in '34 spring training thinner than Bill Powell— and won 26 games and lost five for an .839 percentage, the best I ever hung up.

Anyway, on Setember 29, 1932, wen I went against Lon Warneke and the Cubs, I was thin and felt good.

I had a break, for Warneke showed up wild and kept putting men on for us to bat around, while I found I could get the ball where I wanted and where the Cubs didn't. That afternoon I fanned eight and walked only one. Guy Bush had been wild in the first game of the series and in these first two games we got 10 walks which turned into nine runs.

As I remember it, the Cubs didn't even threaten mildly after tying the score in the third, for we went ahead with a couple more in our half and wound up winning 5–2.

It wasn't any closeness of score or suspense that made it my biggest baseball day; it was simply that it was my first World Series game and I won it.

I remember Gabby Hartnett hitting one down the left field line and Ben Chapman, the fastest man in the American League, scooping up the ball and firing it to second in time for Crosetti to be waiting with it when the old "Milford Freight" came steaming into the bag.

When the rest of the Yanks got through slapping ol' Lon around about all he had left was his chaw of terbacker. And even that was pretty well used up. But if I didn't hit Lon he didn't hit me. So I guess we're even in that respect.

That one game was my only chance in the '32 Series. The Babe fixed the third one up for us in Chicago by waving toward the bleachers in center field and then whacking one of Charley Root's pitches in there. Pipgras pitched us to a 7–5 win, and the next day Wilcy Moore beat Bush, Warneke, Jakie May, Bud Tinning and a great many other gentlemen whose names escape me, 13–6.

The whole Series was pretty enjoyable for me. I was going with June O'Dea, prima donna of the Broadway show, "Of Thee I Sing," at the time and, hanging around the theater saw the show so often I felt I could act myself. So when bookers came to me after the series I signed up without a quiver for vaudeville monologues on a 12-week booking. I lasted three weeks, but the audiences didn't.

I knew so little about show business that one afternoon at Loew's State in New York, when the manager said, "There won't be anybody here for the supper show," I started to skip that show as a matter of course. He caught me as I was leaving for the Rodeo over at Madison Square Garden and drove me back into my dressing room, where I put on my Yankee uniform and went out and gave my monologue to three stews, two of whom were asleep when I started and the third soon was.

The year 1932 I am safe in saying saw an end to my career in the theater.

ROGERS HORNSBY

as told to Bill Van Fleet

The greatest National League batter of 'em all! Rogers Hornsby, born April 27, 1896, in Winters, Texas, conducted a reign of terror against pitchers which lasted 23 years. He hit .424 in 1924, the highest seasonal batting mark ever recorded in modern baseball history. He also led the National League in batting seven times. The Rajah played with the Cardinals, Braves, Giants, Cubs in the National League, and the Browns in the American. He also managed the Browns for five years. In the last decade of his life Hornsby served as a coach for a number of clubs, including the Mets in their first year. He died in 1963.

THE PEAK of my whole baseball career came in that seventh game of the 1926 World Series. That game, and that Series, is an old, old story by now because it has been told so often, but that day always will be my greatest. As playing manager of the Cardinals, I won St. Louis' first pennant in history and beat one of the finest of all Yankee teams in the same year. You couldn't ask for anything more to remember.

Mechanically, I may say right here, I played a very ordinary game. I got two singles, but neither figured in the scoring. I handled five chances without an error, but not one was a hard play. So it wasn't what I did, but what WE did, as a championship team, that will never be forgotten. Personally, I came as close to being one of the all-time goats as eventually winding up with the temporary rank of first-class hero.

Just to start from the beginning, our club was rated well from opening day that season, but for a long time we couldn't get going. We really didn't move into contention for the flag until early in September. With about two weeks to go we won two out of three from the Reds and went into the lead, but then lost three out of four in Boston and fell into second place. In Philly we rallied for five out of six and it was September 27, or thereabouts, that we beat the Giants a doubleheader to clinch the title. This was the team destined to outfinish the mighty Ruth and Gehrig and Bob Meusel and Lazzeri.

No question but what fandom was pulling for us. We were the newcomers to championship circles. We were brash Davids throwing rocks at the Yankee Goliaths and nobody can say we didn't give 'em a battle. The only real "cleaning" we got was the day in St. Louis when Ruth hit those three homers to score four runs and drive in four more. The other Yank wins were by Herb Pennock, 2–1 and 3–2, while Jess Haines and old Pete Alexander packed away three for us. It was Alex who had simply breezed to a 10–2 triumph in No. 6. Old Pete didn't have to bear down at all and suddenly we were at the climax. It was now or never for both. There'd be no tomorrow for either. Jess Haines, who had hurled the only shutout of the Series in whipping "Dutch" Reuther, was my choice; Waite Hoyt drew the Yankee assignment. You can imagine the scene in Yankee Stadium. The very air tingled. You couldn't step on that field without experiencing a feeling that this whole setup was a grand, grand thing.

The Yanks got a run in the first. We got three in the fourth on singles by Tommy Thevenow, "Chick" Hafey and Jim Bottomley, thanks to a couple of timely Yank misplays. Even when Joe Dungan's single and a two-bagger by Hank Severeid gave the American Leaguers another run in the sixth, I didn't particularly worry. Haines was the kind of a pitcher who could hang onto a one-run lead if it came down to it. Then he unaccountably grew wild. Standing back there as he walked the first man in the seventh I wondered if, finally, the strain was beginning to tell.

With two out, he walked three men to fill the bases. I was thinking he ought to get one out of four out, even with Lazzeri up, then I figured something had happened to Jess. I walked over to him and asked. It had. A blister had broken on the first finger from the pressure of throwing his knuckler. Because he couldn't roll the ball over that raw spot without flinching a bit, he'd lost control. We were in a tight spot. Bases full of Yanks and a fellow waiting to hit who might have extended Haines even when Jess was in perfect shape. I made the only choice I could; the only selection any manager could make. I called Alexander.

It was no spot for youth and sheer speed even if I'd had some in the bull pen. You couldn't throw the ball past the Yanks then any more than in recent years. You couldn't afford to make a mistake in this clutch and the only man available was Alex. You should have heard the rumbling through the stands.

One minute the fans had seen Alex sitting in the sun out yonder, apparently oblivious to what was going on; the next he was shambling toward the mound, the biggest man in America . . . the man of the day and the hour and the moment. What the fans didn't know was that Alex never warmed up much. He never had to. He took his time getting to the hill and, of course, what I said to him and what he answered has been written before. "We're in a tough spot," I told him, "and there's no place to put this guy." He twisted his lips into that slow, tilted smile and nodded in complete understanding of the situation as he replied: "I'll take care of that," just like he was accepting a chore to do for an old friend.

There are a few things I'd like to say about Alexander. Almost every fan has heard stories of that game, about how he still was reeling from a celebration the night before and a lot of other things. Some fans have even told me, to my face, that I had to send a cab to get him out of a barroom after the game had started. That, of course, was a downright lie. After the sixth game some friends picked Alex up and they had a few drinks at a hotel. That was only natural, and I knew where they were. But Alex was as sober as I was for the final game and everybody who knows me knows I never took a drink in my life. He never gave me a bit of trouble.

Well, there was Alex in the sunlight and there was Lazzeri. There were the base-runners straining at leashes. There was that great crowd just about smothered by the tenseness of the spot. I moved back to position and waited. The first pitch came in low and inside, a curve. As Alex threw I couldn't help noticing the honest-to-God elegance . . . that's the only word to describe it . . . with which he pitched. He was more than graceful . . . he was a gesture of perfection itself. Just the same, Lazzeri swung and got his meat-end of the bat around in time. The ball sailed for the left-field bleachers and my heart came as close to stopping as it ever will before it never beats again.

It curved foul. Not by much. No more than two feet at the most. We had been given a new lease on life; the title hadn't yet slipped out of reach. As if the pitch was something Alex had to get out of his system before he could go about his work, he mowed down Tony on two more tosses and the danger was over. The greatest pitcher of them all didn't allow a ball hit out of the infield the next two innings, but there still was a little excitement in the guise of anticlimax to come. Ruth came up in the ninth with two out and nobody on.

The count reached three and two and the Babe chose to let the sixth pitch go by. Umpire Bill Klem called it a ball and for a minute there was an argument at the plate. Bob O'Farrell, our catcher, thought it caught a corner, but, of course, the decision stood, and Meusel was next. Nobody ever doubted but what he could blast with the best on occasion. We were scared all over again, but the Yanks came to our rescue. They decided to let Ruth run.

He went down on the first pitch just to make the surprise move as effective as possible, but O'Farrell's throw had him by 10 feet. I'll always remember putting the ball on him. He didn't say a word. He didn't even look around or up at me. He just picked himself off the ground and walked away to the dugout and I had lived through the greatest day any man could ask.

KING CARL HUBBELL

as told to John P. Carmichael

Carl Owen Hubbell, born June 22, 1903, in Carthage, Missouri, was a gangling, rawboned southpaw who threw a deceptive screwball with matchless control, and was the mound perfectionist of the middle '30s. He led the New York Giants to three pennants and occupies a hallowed spot among Polo Ground immortals. King Carl faced his last batter in 1943, and is now chief of the San Francisco farm system.

I CAN remember Frankie Frisch coming off the field behind me at the end of the third inning, grunting to Bill Terry: "I could play second base 15 more years behind that guy. He doesn't need any help. He does it all by himself." Then we hit the bench, and Terry slapped me on the arm and said: "That's pitching, boy!" and Gabby Hartnett let his mask fall down and yelled at the American League dugout: "We gotta look at that all season," and I was pretty happy.

As far as control and "stuff" is concerned, I never had any more in my life than for that All-Star game in 1934. But I never was a strikeout pitcher like Bob Feller or "Dizzy" Dean or "Dazzy" Vance. My style of pitching was to make the other team hit the ball, but on the ground. It was as big a surprise to me to strike out all those fellows as it probably was to them. Before the game, Hartnett and I went down the lineup . . . Gehringer, Manush, Ruth, Gehrig, Foxx, Simmons, Cronin, Dickey and Gomez. There wasn't a pitcher they'd ever faced that they hadn't belted one off him somewhere, sometime.

We couldn't discuss weaknesses . . . they didn't have any, except the screwball. Get that over, but keep your fast ball and hook outside. We can't let 'em hit in the air." So that's the way we started. I knew I had only three innings to work and could bear down on every pitch.

They talk about those All-Star games being exhibition affairs and maybe they are, but I've seen very few players in my life who didn't want to win, no matter whom they were playing or what for. If I'm playing cards for pennies, I want to win. How can you feel any other way? Besides, there were 50,000 fans or more there, and they wanted to see the best you've got. There was an obligation to the people, as well as to ourselves, to go all out. I can recall walking out to the hill in the Polo Grounds that day and looking around the stands and thinking to myself: "Hub, they want to see what you've got."

Gehringer was first up and Hartnett called for a waste ball just so I'd get the feel of the first pitch. It was a little too close, and Charley singled. Down from one of the stands came a yell: "Take him out!"

I had to laugh.

Terry took a couple of steps off first and hollered: "That's all right," and there was Manush at the plate. If I recollect rightly, I got two strikes on him, but then he refused to swing any more, and I lost him. He walked. This time Terry and Frisch and "Pie" Traynor and Travis Jackson all came over to the mound and began worrying. "Are you all right?" Bill asked me. I assured him I was. I could hear more than one voice now from the stands: "Take him out before it's too late."

Well, I could imagine how they felt with two on, nobody out and Ruth at bat. To strike him out was the last thought in my mind. The thing was to make him hit on the ground. He wasn't too fast, as you know, and he'd be a cinch to double. He never took the bat off his shoulder. You could have pushed me over with your little finger. I fed him three straight screwballs, all over the plate, after wasting a fast ball, and he stood there. I can see him looking at the umpire on "You're out," and he wasn't mad. He just didn't believe it, and Hartnett was laughing when he threw the ball back.

So up came Gehrig. He was a sharp hitter. You could double him, too, now and then, if the ball was hit hard and straight at an infielder. That's what we hoped he'd do, at best. Striking out Ruth and Gehrig in succession was too big an order. By golly, he fanned . . . and on four pitches. He swung at the last screwball, and you should have heard that crowd. I felt a lot easier then, and even when Gehringer and Manush pulled a double steal and got to third and second, with Foxx up, I looked down at Hartnett and caught the screwball sign, and Jimmy missed. We were really trying to strike Foxx out, with two already gone, and Gabby didn't bother to waste any pitches. I threw three more screwballs, and he went down swinging. We had set down the side on 12 pitches, and then Frisch hit a homer in our half of the first, and we were ahead.

It was funny, when I thought of it afterwards, how Ruth and Gehrig looked as they stood there. The Babe must have been waiting for me to get the ball up a little so he could get his bat under it. He always was trying for that one big shot at the stands, and anything around his knees, especially a twisting ball, didn't let him get any leverage. Gehrig apparently decided to take one swing at least and he beat down at the pitch, figuring to take a chance on being doubled if he could get a piece of the ball. He whispered something to Foxx as Jim got up from the batter's circle and while I didn't hear it, I found out later he said: "You might as well cut . . . it won't get any higher." At least Foxx wasted no time.

Of course the second inning was easier because Simmons and Cronin both struck out with nobody on base and then I got too close to Dickey and he singled. Simmons and Foxx, incidentally, both went down swinging and I know every pitch to them was good enough to hit at and those they missed had a big hunk of the plate. Once Hartnett kinda shook his head at me as if to say I was getting too good. After Dickey came Gomez and as he walked into the box he looked down at Gabby and said: "You are now looking at a man whose batting average is .104. What the hell am I doing up here?" He was easy after all those other guys and we were back on the bench again.

We were all feeling pretty good by this time and Traynor began counting on his fingers: "Ruth, Gehrig, Foxx, Simmons, Cronin! Hey, Hub, do you put anything on the ball?"

THE BOX SCORE
(July 10, 1934)

NATIONAL LEAGUE	A.B.	R.	H.	P.	A.		AMERICAN LEAGUE	A.B.	R.	H.	P.	A.
Frisch, 2b.	3	3	2	0	1		Gehringer, 2b.	3	0	2	2	1
W. Herman, 2b.	2	0	1	0	1		Manush, lf.	2	0	0	0	0
Traynor, 3b.	5	2	2	1	0		Ruffing, p.	1	0	1	0	0
Medwick, lf.	2	1	1	0	0		Harder, p.	2	0	0	1	0
Klein, lf.	3	0	1	1	0		Ruth, rf.	2	1	0	0	0
Cuyler, rf.	2	0	0	2	0		Chapman, rf.	2	0	1	0	1
Ott, rf.	2	0	0	0	1		Gehrig, 1b.	4	1	0	11	1
Berger, cf.	2	0	0	0	0		Foxx, 3b.	5	1	2	1	2
P. Waner, cf.	2	0	0	1	0		Simmons, cf.-lf.	5	3	3	3	0
Terry, 1b.	3	0	1	4	0		Cronin, ss.	5	1	2	2	8
Jackson, ss.	2	0	0	0	1		Dickey, c.	2	1	1	4	0
Vaughan, ss.	2	0	0	4	0		Cochrane, c.	1	0	0	1	1
Hartnett, c.	2	0	0	9	0		Gomez, p.	1	0	0	0	0
Lopez, c.	2	0	0	5	1		Averill, cf.	4	1	2	1	0
Hubbell, p.	0	0	0	0	0		West, cf.	0	0	0	1	0
Warneke, p.	0	0	0	0	0							
Mungo, p.	0	0	0	0	0							
Martin	0	1	0	0	0							
J. Dean, p.	1	0	0	0	0							
Frankhouse, p.	1	0	0	0	0							
Totals	36	7	8	27	5		Totals	39	9	14	27	14

W. Herman batted for Hubbell in 3rd and took Frisch's place in 7th.

Klein batted for Medwick in 5th.

Ott batted for Cuyler in 5th.

P. Waner batted for Berger in 5th.

Vaughan batted for Jackson in 5th.

Martin batted for Mungo in 5th.

Cochrane ran for Dickey in 6th.
Averill batted for Gomez in 4th.

AMERICAN LEAGUE	0 0 0 2 6 1 0 0 0—9
NATIONAL LEAGUE	1 0 3 0 3 0 0 0 0—7

Errors—Berger, Gehrig. Runs batted in—Frisch, Medwick (3), Cronin (2), Averill (3), Foxx, Simmons, Ruffing. Two-base hits—Simmons (2), Averill, Cronin, Foxx, W. Herman. Three-base hits—Averill, Chapman. Home runs—Frisch, Medwick. Stolen bases—Gehringer, Manush, Traynor, Ott. Double play—Lopez and Vaughan. Bases on balls—Off Hubbell 2, Gomez 1, Warneke 3, Mungo 2, Ruffing 1, J. Dean 1, Harder 1, Frankhouse 1. Struck out—By Hubbell 6, Gomez 3, Warneke 1, Mungo 1, Harder 2, J. Dean 4. Pitching records—Hubbell, 2 hits, 0 runs in three innings; Warneke, 2 hits, 2 runs in 1 (none out in fifth); Mungo, 4 hits, 6 runs in 1; J. Dean, 5 hits, 1 run in 3; Gomez, 3 hits, 4 runs in 3; Ruffing, 4 hits, 2 runs in 1 (none out in fifth). Left on bases—American League—12. National League—5. Winning pitcher—Harder. Losing pitcher—Mungo. Umpires—Pittman (N. L.); Moriarity (A. L.); Owens (A. L.); Stark (N. L.). Time of game—2:44.

Terry came over to see how my arm was, but it never was stronger. I walked one man in the third . . . don't remember who it was . . . but this time Ruth hit one on the ground and we were still all right. You could hear him puff when he swung. That was all for me. Afterwards, they got six runs in the fifth and licked us, but for three innings I had the greatest day in my life. One of the writers who kept track told me that I'd pitched 27 strikes and 21 balls to 13 men and only five pitches were hit in fair territory.

WALTER JOHNSON

as told to John P. Carmichael

What a pitcher was Walter Perry Johnson! Born on November 6, 1887, in Humboldt, Kansas, the "Big Train" whipped his smoke ball past American League batters for 21 years, all with the Washington Senators. He struck out more men than any other pitcher, 3497, and his total of 414 games won is second only to Cy Young. A huge and gentle man who was always frightened that one of his serves might accidentally strike a batter and result in severe injury, Johnson was extra careful with his control and walked very few batters. After his glorious pitching career was finished, Walter managed at Washington and Cleveland. Then he retired to his Maryland farm where he became a leader in local politics before he died on December 10, 1946.

("As the hitter sees Johnson's arm descending, just swing," said Outfielder "Birdie" Cree years ago. "The bat will then cross the plate at about the same time the ball reaches it and, if you're lucky, you hit the ball. A fellow does not have to judge the height of the pitch . . . or if it was a curve.")

THIS WON'T be very original, I'm afraid (said Johnson) because there couldn't be a bigger day for me than the one everybody knows about . . . October 10, 1924, in the last game of my first World Series. It was Weiser, Idaho, and Detroit and Washington put together; I guess you'd call it a piece of every day for 18 years and it didn't look like I'd ever see it come around. After all, I was 36 years old and that's pretty far gone to be walking into the last game of a series . . . especially when you couldn't blame people for remembering I'd lost two starts already.

You see I didn't have much besides a fast ball in my life and there comes a time when speed alone won't stop a batter. If a boy hasn't got real, natural speed it isn't worth his while to try and force a fast ball, because a slow pitch and a curve can fool a hitter better than unnatural speed. Besides, the arm may suffer. A free, loose motion and control are the main assets for a pitcher. That's all I ever had to amount to anything.

Why, when I started out at 18 years of age I couldn't even land a job on the Pacific Coast. I went to Weiser, Idaho, because it had a semipro team and the players worked in the mines. I won my first game 4–0 on two hits. I won the next 2–1 in 15 innings and then fanned 15 to make my string three straight.

Weiser people began calling me "pardner" instead of "sonny." I still was at Weiser in 1907 and had won 13 and lost 2 when Cliff Blankenship, a Washington scout, arrived. He'd really come out to look at Clyde Milan; I was just a by-product of his trip.

Well, he never saw me pitch at all, but he knew my record and offered me a job. I wouldn't take it until he'd promised me a return ticket to California in case I failed. I joined Washington at Detroit August 2, 1907, despite the pleas of Weiser folk who offered to buy me a cigar stand and set me up in business if I'd stay there. But you know how you are at 18 . . . you want to see things.

I saw something my first start. I got beat 3–2 and Ty Cobb and Sam Crawford bunted me all over the infield. I fell all over myself . . . and the 1,000 people in the stands laughed themselves sick. I was so confused I even missed the bus back to the hotel . . . and was walking there in my uniform when some fans gave me a lift.

Seventeen years later I was in a series, but I wasn't happy about it. I'd been beaten in New York for the second time by the Giants and I'll admit when I got on the train to Washington, where we were to play the seventh game, there were tears in my eyes. I was carrying my youngest boy on my shoulder and trying not to speak to people when Clark

Griffith put a hand on my arm. "Don't think about it any-more, Walter," he told me. "You're a great pitcher. We all know it.

"Now tonight when we get home don't stand around the box offices buying seats for friends or shaking hands with people who feel sorry for you. I've seen many a fast ball shaken right out of a pitcher's hand. Go home and get to bed early . . . we may need you tomorrow." I told him I would.

You can imagine how "red hot" Washington was next day . . . the last game of its first World Series coming up. Thirty-five thousand people were crammed into our park. President Coolidge was there. I made myself as inconspicuous as possible on the bench, because I didn't want any sympathy . . . and I didn't even want Harris to think of me in a jam. Well, "Bucky" started Curley Ogden but pretty soon George Mogridge was in there and then "Firpo" Marberry, our big relief ace.

We were all tied up in the ninth when I came in. I'll always believe that Harris gambled on me because of sentiment, but he said no. He just told me: "You're the best we got, Walter . . . we've got to win or lose with you." So I walked out there and it seemed to me the smoke from the stands was so thick on the field that nobody could see me. I remembered thinking: "I'll need the breaks" and if I didn't actually pray, I sort of was thinking along those lines.

I was in trouble every inning. After getting Fred Lindstrom in the ninth, Frank Frisch hit a fast ball to right center for three bases. We decided to pass Ross Young and then I struck out George Kelly and "Irish" Meusel grounded to third. In the 10th I walked "Hack" Wilson and then, after striking out Travis Jackson, I was lucky enough to grab a drive by ol' Hank Gowdy and turn it into a double play.

Heinie Groh batted for Hugh McQuillan, the Giant pitcher, in the 11th and singled. Lindstrom bunted him along. I fanned Frisch, this time, on an outside pitch and once more passed Young. Kelly struck out again.

They kept after me, though. Meusel singled in the 12th, but I'd settled down to believe, by then, that maybe this was my day and I got the next three hitters. I'd tried to win my own game in the 10th with a long ball to the wall, but Wilson pulled it down. So I was up again in the 12th when it was getting pretty dark. "Muddy" Ruel had lifted a pop foul to Gowdy, who lost it, and on the next pitch Ruel hit past third for two bases. Then I sent an easy grounder to short . . . and Jackson fumbled. We all sat there

THE BOX SCORE
(October 10, 1924)

NEW YORK	A.B.	R.	H.	P.	A.	WASHINGTON	A.B.	R.	H.	P.	A.
Lindstrom, 3b.	5	0	1	0	3	McNeely, cf.	6	0	1	0	0
Frisch, 2b.	5	0	2	3	4	Harris, 2b.	5	1	3	4	1
Young, rf.-lf.	2	1	0	2	0	Rice, cf.	5	0	0	2	0
Kelly, cf.-1b.	6	1	1	8	1	Goslin, lf.	5	0	2	3	0
Terry, 1b.	2	0	0	6	1	Judge, 1b.	4	0	1	11	1
Meusel, lf.-rf.	3	0	1	1	0	Bluege, ss.	5	0	0	1	7
Wilson, lf.-cf.	5	1	1	4	0	Taylor, 3b.	2	0	0	0	3
Jackson, ss.	6	0	0	1	4	Miller, 3b.	2	0	0	1	1
Gowdy, c.	6	0	1	8	0	Ruel, c.	5	2	2	13	0
Barnes, p.	4	0	0	1	2	Ogden, p.	0	0	0	0	0
McQuillan, p.	0	0	0	0	0	Mogridge, p.	1	0	0	0	0
Nehf, p.	0	0	0	0	0	Marberry, p.	1	0	0	1	0
Bentley, p.	0	0	0	0	0	Johnson, p.	2	0	0	0	1
Groh	1	0	1	0	0	Tate	0	0	0	0	0
Southworth	0	0	0	0	0	Shirley	0	0	0	0	0
						Leibold	1	1	1	0	0
Totals	45	3	8	*34	15	Totals	44	4	10	36	14

Meusel batted for Terry in 6th.
Groh batted for McQuillan in 11th.
Southworth ran for Groh in 11th.
* One out when winning run was scored.

Tate batted for Marberry in 8th.
Shirley ran for Tate in 8th.
Leibold batted for Taylor in 8th.

NEW YORK	0	0	0	0	0	3	0	0	0	0	0	0—3
WASHINGTON	0	0	0	1	0	0	0	2	0	0	0	1—4

Errors—Jackson (2), Gowdy, Judge, Bluege (2), Taylor. Earned runs—Washington 4, New York 1. Runs batted in—Harris 3, McNeely 1, Meusel 1. Two-base hits—McNeely, Goslin, Ruel, Leibold, Lindstrom. Three-base hit—Frisch. Home run—Harris. Double plays—Kelly to Jackson, Jackson to Frisch to Kelly, Johnson to Bluege to Judge. Bases on balls—Off Ogden 1, Mogridge 1, Marberry 1, Bentley 1, Barnes 1, Johnson 3. Struck out—By Ogden 1, Mogridge 3, Marberry 3, McMillan 1, Barnes 6, Johnson 5. Hits—Off Ogden 0 in 1-3 inning, Mogridge 4 in 4 2-3 innings, Marberry 1 in 3 innings, Johnson 3 in 4 innings, Barnes 6 in 7 2-3 innings, Nehf 1 in 2-3 inning, McQuillan 0 in 1 2-3 innings, Bentley 3 in 1 1-3 innings (one out in 12th). Winning pitcher—Johnson. Losing pitcher—Bentley. Umpires—Dinneen (A); Quigley (N), Connolly (A), Klem (N). Time—3:00.

staring at Earl McNeely as he hit an easy grounder to Lindstrom.

The ball never touched Fred. It hit a pebble and arched over his head into safe territory. I could feel tears smarting in my eyes as Ruel came home with the winning run. I'd won. We'd won. I felt so happy that it didn't seem real. They told me in the clubhouse that President Coolidge kept watching me all the way into the clubhouse and I remember somebody yelling: "I bet Cal'd like to change places with you right now, Walter."

A long time later Mrs. Johnson and I slipped away to a quiet little restaurant where I used to eat on Vermont Avenue, in Washington, and do you know that before we were through with our dinner 200 telegrams had been delivered there. I never thought so many people were pulling for me to win, because the Giants were pretty popular. When we packed up and went home to Kansas we had three trunks full of letters from fans all over the world.

HARMON KILLEBREW

as told by Jack Orr

Harmon Clayton Killebrew, born June 29, 1936 at Payette, Idaho, may be the most underrated home run slugger of his time. Seldom does he get the headlines his fellow American League bruisers do, possibly because he is a reticent type and more probably because the teams he has played for in Washington and Minnesota captured only one pennant in his lifetime. But Killebrew's credentials are very much in order. He has been named to the All-Star squad nine times since he became a big leaguer and he has led his league in homers five times. He joined the Senators when he was only 18, fresh from the College of Idaho (Caldwell). He is preparing for a post-career position as an insurance executive in off-seasons.

ONE OF the astonishing little-known facts about Harm Killebrew, the man they call "Killer," is that after the 1967 season he had hit more home runs at his age (31) than the fabled Babe Ruth hit at the same age. Ruth accounted for 356 big ones in a 13-year period when he first broke in; Killebrew smacked 380. Of course the Babe played for another nine years and amassed enough to establish the all-time major league record of 714, so Killebrew has his work cut out for him in the next decade. The Twins' slugger's mark to date also surpasses the number of homers in a comparable period hit by such luminaries as Ted Williams, Willie Mays, Roger Maris, Jimmy Foxx, Ralph Kiner and Hank Greenberg.

In the nine-year stretch, between 1959 and 1967, Killebrew hit 40 or more home runs six times. He led the American League in slugging percentage twice and drove in 100 or more runs on six occasions.

Ralph Kiner, who in an eleven-year career hit fewer homers than Killebrew already has hit, has said that Harm has the best chance among active players today to reach the stupendous all-time Ruthian mark. "He has more potential than the others. He seldom is injured. And I believe he is a better hitter now (1967) than he ever was."

One cross big Harm has had to bear in the big leagues was the constant switching from one position to another, hardly conducive to steady performance. As a rookie he came in as a second baseman, and for several years he alternated at that position and at third, with so-so defensive marks. By 1958 he was a third baseman and left fielder, but two years later he was spotted at third, in left and at first base, the first time he had tried that post. He continued to whirl around the diamond until the Twins picked up Vic Power, a dandy first baseman, and Killebrew was directed to left field again. When Power left the game, it was back to the old left-first-third shuffle for the Killer and he performed uncomplainingly at each job. These were the years when Killebrew was delivering his forty-plus homers annually and he was a tough man to keep on the bench.

By the season of 1967, Don Mincher, who had been holding down first base for the Twins, went to the California Angels in the swap for Dean Chance, and the Minnesota powers-that-be handed down a notice that from that point on, Killebrew was the first sacker, period.

The move worked out well. The compact Killer (six-feet, 200 pounds) played 160 of his 163 games at first base and it seemed to help his hitting considerably. He tied for the league leadership in home runs (44) with the league's Most Valuable Player, Carl Yastrzemski, was second in runs-batted-in (113 to Yaz's 121) and was runner-up, again to Yaz, in slugging percentage.

Killebrew's lone World Series, in 1965, is not one he likes to remember. Though he smashed one gigantic home run off Don Drysdale and though the Twins did make the Dodgers scramble through seven games before they won, Harm only hit .286, driving in only two runs.

But in All-Star competition, he is unique in that he was selected for the American League squad no less than nine

times—and at three different positions. His fellow professionals voted him to the third base position starting in 1959
and then made him their choice for left field in 1963 and
1964. Then, as a first baseman, he made the All-Stars three
years in a row, 1965, 1966 and 1967. He has established a
tidy .300 batting average in All-Star competition.

But the one aspect of hitting which has intrigued Kille-
brew-watchers over the years is the distances the balls he
slams travel. It has intrigued Killebrew himself, and when
he does answer questions in interviews he is likely to mention the length of some of his historic clouts.

In 1962 he lambasted a ball clear over the roof at Detroit's
Tiger Stadium, a blast well over 450 feet, and the only one
before or since to be hit over the left field stand. On his
first visit to the California Angels' new stadium in Anaheim,
California, in 1966, he hit one to the base of the scoreboard,
almost a 500-foot drive. He once hit four monstrous homers
in a single day—a doubleheader on September 21, 1963.

The one most people talk about, however, came on June 3,
1967, at Minnesota's Metropolitan Stadium in a game
against the California Angels. It was a 3–1 ball game in
favor of the Twins when Killebrew stepped in against Lew
Burdette with two men on. The count went to 3–2 and
then Burdette delivered—and the Killer killed it. The ball
soared into the second deck of the bleachers beyond the
left field fence and splintered a seat six rows deep in that
upper tier. It was the first ball ever hit upstairs in the
history of the Minneapolis park. Everyone who saw it agreed
that the ball would have gone well over 500 feet in the air
if it hadn't been stopped by the second deck. The Twins'
publicity man, Tom Mee, later did some calculating with
distance and height and concluded the smash would have
gone 530 feet. Killebrew conceded that he "hit it pretty
good." His teammates were still in awe after the game (won
by the Twins as the result of Killer's muscle), and one said,
"Five-hundred-thirty-feet, my neck. More like five-hundred-
thirty-yards."

Minnesota management also was impressed and for the
first time in baseball history a shattered seat was "retired."
It was painted orange to mark the range and was never sold
again. It stands like a beacon for the amusement and de-
light of early-arrivals at the park.

On the following day, off the Angels' Jack Sanford, Kille-

THE BOX SCORE
(June 3, 1967)

CALIFORNIA	A.B.	R.	H.	RBI.
Cardenal, cf.	5	0	1	0
Schaal, 3b.	2	1	2	0
Fregosi, ss.	4	0	1	1
Mincher, 1b.	4	2	2	0
Hall, rf.	4	1	0	0
Reichardt, lf.	5	1	2	3
Satriano, c.	5	1	2	2
Knoop, 2b.	4	0	1	0
M'F'lane, ph.	1	0	0	0
Brunet, p.	1	0	0	0
Burdette, p.	0	0	0	0
J'nstone, ph.	1	0	0	0
Coates, p.	0	0	0	0
Morton, ph.	1	0	1	0
Kelso, p.	0	0	0	0
Rojas, p.	0	0	0	0
Skowron, ph.	1	0	1	0
Wallace, pr.	0	0	0	0
Cimino, p.	0	0	0	0
Totals	**38**	**6**	**13**	**6**

MINNESOTA	A.B.	R.	H.	RBI.
Tovar, cf.	3	0	2	0
Uhl'nder, cf.	0	1	0	0
Carew, 2b.	4	3	2	1
Rollins, 3b.	3	2	2	0
Kil'brew, 1b.	3	1	1	3
Allison, lf.	4	0	1	3
Val'pino, rf.	3	0	1	0
Versalles, ss.	4	0	1	1
Zim'rman, c.	3	0	0	0
Boswell, p.	2	1	0	0
Ollum, p.	0	0	0	0
Perry, p.	1	0	1	0
Nixon, ph.	1	0	0	0
Kline, p.	0	0	0	0
Totals	**31**	**8**	**11**	**8**

```
CALIFORNIA    0 0 1  0 0 4  0 0 1—6
MINNESOTA     0 0 2  4 0 0  0 2 x—8
```

CALIFORNIA

	IP.	H.	R.	ER.	BB.	SO.
Brunet (L. 1-9)	3⅔	7	4	4	3	2
Burdette	⅓	1	2	2	0	0
Coates	1	1	0	0	0	1
Kelso	2	1	0	0	3	3
Rojas	⅓	1	2	2	3	0
Cimino	⅔	0	0	0	0	1

MINNESOTA

	IP.	H.	R.	ER.	BB.	SO.
Boswell (W. 2-3)	5*	6	4	4	4	5
Ollum	0†	2	1	1	0	0
Perry	2	2	0	1	1	1
Kline (Save 1)	2	3	1	1	1	2

*Pitched to three batters in sixth.
†Pitched to two batters in sixth.

E—None. DP—California 1, Minnesota 1. LOB—California 11, Minnesota 12. 2B—Schaal, Rollins, Allison, Mincher 2, Satriano. HR—Killebrew (11), Reichardt (5), Satriano (2). SH—Zimmerman, Rollins. HBP—By Burdette (Rollins), by Cimino (Versalles). PB—Satriano 2. U—Honochick, Chylak, Haller and Drummond. T—3:27. A—12,337.

brew hit one almost as far, a liner which bounced off the facing of the same second deck, one section farther toward center field than the first one.

That broken seat stands as Harmon Clayton ,Killebrew's monument, to date. But if he continues to splinter fences until he reaches age 40, as the Babe and Ted Williams did before him, the monument will most surely be a new page in the record book.

SANDY KOUFAX

as told by Jack Orr

In the last five years of a superb baseball career, Sandy Koufax, despite a crippling arthritic condition, was the best pitcher in the world. In those five years (1962 through 1966) he won 111 games, lost only 34, limited opponents to less than two runs a game, set an unparalleled strikeout mark, won four World Series games (two by shutouts) and threw four no-hitters, more than anyone in history. His arm ailment forced retirement after the 1966 season when he was thirty-one and still at his peak. Sandy is now a $100,000-a-year television sports broadcaster for the National Broadcasting Company.

WHEN THE Brooklyn Dodgers pulled up stakes in 1957 and moved to Los Angeles, Sandy Koufax was just a so-so member of a pitching corps that included names such as Don Newcombe, Don Drysdale, Carl Erskine, Clem Labine, Roger Craig and Johnny Podres. Koufax was only twenty-two and his record wasn't particularly promising. In three years in Brooklyn he had won 9 games and lost 10; he was often wild, and he had a mysterious twinge in his shoulder which doctors were unable to diagnose.

But in the decade that followed, Koufax blossomed into the game's most outstanding pitcher. He helped the Dodgers win four pennants and three world's championships. He was named the National League's Most Valuable Player in 1963 and three times won the Cy Young Memorial Award, symbolic of the best pitcher in baseball. He established remarkable strikeout records, twice tying the all-time record of 18 in one game, breaking the all-time season strikeout record (382 in 1965) and becoming the only pitcher ever to average more than a strikeout an inning (2396 in 2325 innings pitched).

Surprisingly, Koufax always said that he did not gun for a heavy strikeout total. "The only time I really try for a strikeout," he once said, "is when I'm in a jam. If the bases are loaded with none out, for example, then I'll go for the strikeout. But most of the time I try to throw to spots. I try to get them to pop up or ground out. On a strikeout I might have to throw five or six pitches, sometimes more if there are foul-offs. That tires me. So I just try to get outs. That's what counts: outs. You win with outs, not strikeouts."

Nevertheless, the Brooklyn-born Koufax, who wasn't even a baseball fan as a teenager (he wanted to be an architect), became the strikeout king of his generation. And many people said that only his early retirement kept him from approaching the glamorous all-time record of 3,508 whiffed batsmen, set by Walter Johnson over a 21-year period in the first quarter of the century.

Over his own dozen years in the majors, Koufax amassed a glittering catalogue of unforgettable games. Many recall his World Series triumphs. Others point to his pair of 18-strikeout games. Others simply remember his painful struggle with his arm on the occasions when even lifting it sent stabbing twinges through his body.

But there can be nothing superior to perfection—and that's what Koufax was on the night of September 9, 1965, in Dodger Stadium, Los Angeles. Sandy pitched the fourth no-hit game of his career and not a Cub batsman reached first base. (In the some 15,000 games played in the major leagues since 1871 there had been only nine perfect games until Koufax's. There had been only one in regular season play in forty-three years—the Phils' Jim Bunning in 1964—and Don Larsen of the Yankees had pitched one in the World Series of 1956.)

On Koufax's day in 1965, it was an important game for the Dodgers. There were less than three weeks left in the pennant race, and Los Angeles was in a dogfight with the San Francisco Giants and the Cincinnati Reds. A big turnout of 29,139 crowded the Dodgers' four-year-old stadium. Opposing Koufax was a 26-year-old lefthander named Bob Hendley, and, as it happened, the game was the most golden moment of Hendley's major league career, too.

For the first six innings the Cub southpaw almost matched Koufax's perfect pitching. He walked one man in the fifth, and the Dodgers, opportunists that they were that year, turned it into a run. Lou Johnson was the man who drew the walk. He was sacrified to second and when he stole third, Cub catcher Chris Krug threw wildly—and Johnson romped home with the game's only run. Two innings later, with two out, Johnson hit an off-speed pitch off the end of his bat for a looping double that landed near the right field foul line. It was the only hit Hendley gave up.

Meanwhile, Koufax was whizzing brilliantly through the Cub lineup. He had very few close calls. Glenn Beckert, the Cub second baseman, popped a foul that landed just barely outside the left field line in the first inning. Rookie Byron Browne lined sharply to Willie Davis in center in the second. But aside from those blows, Koufax was masterful. His curve angled perfectly and his fast ball popped smartly into the catcher's mitt. Once his perfect game was jeopardized when shortstop Maury Wills threw into the dirt on a routine grounder, but first baseman Wes Parker dug it out with finesse to retire the hitter. And once Sandy went to a 3-balls-no-strikes count on Billy Williams, a Cub slugger. But Koufax quickly whipped across two strikes, and then Williams meekly flied to left.

By mid-game the big crowd began to realize that they were part of a page of history. Koufax, rising to the occasion, seemed to grow stronger. He struck out the last six batters to bring his total to 14 of the 27 hitters he faced.

To start the eighth, Ron Santo, one of the Cub sluggers, took a called third strike. Ernie Banks, the All-Star first baseman, went down swinging for the third time, the only time that year he whiffed three times in a game. Rookie Browne also struck out. Then in the ninth Chris Krug swung at a third strike, pinch-hitter Joey Amalfitano went down swinging at three pitches.

That put the question to Harvey Kuenn, another pinch-hitter and onetime American League batting champion. The thousands of fans had been standing for the final two innings, roaring wildly with each pitch. Sandy threw a sharp-breaking curve for the first strike. He missed inside with a fast ball. Then Kuenn took a vicious swing at the next pitch— and missed. Koufax wound up again and threw a wicked fast ball across Kuenn's letters. The Cub swinger missed and it was all over.

For his performance on his greatest day, Koufax was rewarded with a bottle of champagne from Dodger owner Walter O'Malley, a $500 salary bonus and a contract the following year which made him the first pitcher to receive $100,000 for a season's work. It also elevated him to a summit from which it would be an easy step into baseball's Hall of Fame the first year he would be eligible (1972).

When Koufax decided to quit the game in the winter of 1966, sportswriter Jim Murray eulogized: "Koufax was the most brilliant pitcher in history, if not the best. His career glowed with an incandescence not even a Walter Johnson, Mathewson, Grove or Hubbell could match. His durability

THE BOX SCORE
(September 9, 1965)

CHICAGO (N)	A.B.	R.	H.	RBI.	LOS ANGELES (N)	A.B.	R.	H.	RBI.
Young, cf.	3	0	0	0	Wills, ss.	3	0	0	0
Beckert, 2b.	3	0	0	0	Gilliam, 3b.	3	0	0	0
Williams, rf.	3	0	0	0	Kennedy, 3b.	0	0	0	0
Santo, 3b.	3	0	0	0	W. Davis, cf.	3	0	0	0
Banks, 1b.	3	0	0	0	Johnson, lf.	2	1	1	0
Browne, lf.	3	0	0	0	Fairly, rf.	2	0	0	0
Krug, c.	3	0	0	0	Lefebvre, 2b.	3	0	0	0
Kessinger, ss.	2	0	0	0	Tracewski, 2b.	0	0	0	0
Amalfitano, ph.	1	0	0	0	Parker, 1b.	3	0	0	0
Hendley, p.	2	0	0	0	Torborg, c.	3	0	0	0
Kuenn, ph.	1	0	0	0	Koufax, p.	2	0	0	0
Totals	27	0	0	0	Totals	24	1	1	0

CHICAGO	0	0	0	0	0	0	0	0	0—0	
LOS ANGELES	0	0	0	0	1	0	0	0	x—1	

CHICAGO

	IP.	H.	R.	ER.	BB.	SO.
Hendley (L. 2-3)	8	1	1	0	1	3

LOS ANGELES

	IP.	H.	R.	ER.	BB.	SO.
Koufax (W. 22-7)	9	0	0	0	0	14

E—Krug. LOB—Chicago 0, Los Angeles 1. 2B—Johnson. SB—Johnson. SF—Fairly. T—1:43. A—29,139.

was something else. That's what drove Sandy to risk gangrene, amputation, chronic inflammation—everything short of bubonic plague—to keep pitching. . . You go back to Babe Ruth before you begin to get the idea what Sandy Koufax meant to the Grand Old Game. Baseball lost more than a southpaw. Baseball lost a symbol. Baseball lost part of its integrity."

And all that was never better demonstrated than it was the night he pitched the perfect game.

JIM LONBORG

as told by Jack Orr

Jim Lonborg, a tall (six-foot-six), articulate, studious, handsome man, reached baseball fame with lightning-like swiftness. Born in Santa Maria, California, April 16, 1942, he was graduated with a degree in biology from Stanford University and planned to become a doctor. Instead, he began pitching for the Red Sox. After two seasons, in which he lost more than he won, in 1967 he suddenly blossomed into the league's best pitcher as the amazing Sox won their first pennant in 21 years.

To set the stage for Jim Lonborg's greatest day in baseball it becomes necessary to review the glittering success saga of the Boston Red Sox of 1967. They were called the Cinderella team, for after finishing one-half game out of the cellar in 1966, they clawed and scratched their way to the American League pennant on the last afternoon of the season and went on to give the St. Louis Cardinals an awesome fright in a thrill-packed seven-game World Series.

Lonborg's role in the rise of the Red Sox can scarcely be overestimated. By mid-season he had kept the Sox within striking distance by winning eight decisions against two defeats and by taking a substantial lead in total strikeouts. For the last half of the season, he was superb and for the first time in several decades, Boston had a "stopper," a pitcher who could be counted on to snap any threat of a prolonged losing spin. "He has found out how to pitch," said Red Sox pitching coach Sal Maglie, who knew as much about pitching as anybody in the game when he was a star in the National League.

It had not always been thus with Lonborg. He was known around the league as "Gentleman Jim," too timid in the clutch to whiz a ball under a batter's chin. As a result, opposing hitters dug in fiercely against him and were able to stroke his pitches to all corners of the outfield. The result of that, in Lonborg's first two big league seasons, was an earned-run average of more than four runs a game and a won-lost record of 19–27. He struck out more than he walked, but power hitters on opposing teams drooled in anticipation on his day to pitch.

But the polite away-from-the-hitter formula was dropped in spring training of 1967. Lonborg had played winter ball in Venezuela and had arrived at a decision. He was going to throw occasional fast balls around hitters' chins. "Wait and see," he told a Boston baseball writer in the spring. "Keep count of how many batters I hit this year." He also kept count himself, recording hit batsmen on the back of his glove in ink as a continuous reminder of what he was doing out there. His final bag came to nineteen with several dozen near-misses. Soon the message got around the league that Gentleman Jim had become Tiger Jim. With his fast ball and his new determination, few hitters were anxious to take a chance on being brushed back.

In June he came close to a no-hitter, getting as far as one out in the eighth against the Indians. He continued to win the big ones. He finished the year with 22 victories, nine defeats and a substantial total of 245 strikeouts. "It's a physical game I have discovered," said the revitalized Lonborg, who spends his nights off attending concerts by the Boston Symphony Orchestra. "It comes down to challenging a hitter and beating him. Winning is a wonderful feeling. And so is the big money and I suspect the two things go hand in hand."

In the final week of the season, Lonborg pitched three times and won twice, including the momentous final game of the season against Minnesota's brilliant Dean Chance, the game that won it all for the Red Sox. That day, incidentally, October 1, was the only day of the long season which saw Boston in first place.

The Cardinals, Boston's opponent in the World Series, on the other hand, hadn't been out of first place since mid-

June. They had coasted to the pennant and at year's end had a ten and a half game bulge over the Giants.

As the Series started in Boston's Fenway Park, the strong and fleet Cardinals were heavily favored. Experts who had picked the Red Sox to finish deep in the second division still had their reservations. But the fans across the nation had taken the surprise American League victors to their bosom and, if nothing else, Boston was the sentimental favorite of everybody from cab drivers to bank presidents. Along the New England seaboard staid citizens had seldom been as stirred.

Lonborg saw the first game from the bench as the Cardinal ace, Bob Gibson, turned the Sox' bats to taffy, and speedster Lou Brock got four hits, stole two bases and scored both St. Louis runs. The score was 2–1, but the pair of runs were enough for the powerful, all-business Gibson, who scattered six hits among the Sox sluggers.

But Lonborg was even better in the second game at Fenway. He knocked Brock down on the first pitch of the game. Then he effectively threw sinking fast balls and knee-high curves the rest of the way, winning handily, 5–0. For six and two-thirds innings, in fact, Lonborg pitched a perfect game, retiring twenty consecutive batters before walking Curt Flood on a 3–2 pitch. Later, Julian Javier jumped on a high slider and pumped it into the left field corner for a double—the only hit of the day off the Red Sox ace.

As the Series moved to St. Louis' spanking-new stadium, the Cardinals' class began to make itself felt. Nelson Briles outpitched Gary Bell, Brock contributed two more hits, one a magnificent bunt, and the Cardinals had a one-game edge. When they won again in game No. 4 the following day, behind Gibson's dandy five-hitter, the experts and the fans, reluctantly perhaps, were writing Red Sox obituaries.

The fifth game played in St. Louis would have ended the Series, had the Cardinals won, and in fact they were so confident that it was all over and the games remaining to be played in Boston would not be necessary that many of the Cards didn't bother to pack traveling bags before they came to the park.

That turned out to be a mistake. The Cardinals weren't giving Lonborg his due. He pitched a magnificent three-hit game, forcing the Series back to Boston, and in so doing gave 55,000,000 television viewers, 54, 575 Busch Stadium witnesses and Lonborg himself the greatest moment of that storied season.

This was perhaps the most absorbing game of the Series. The Cardinals used a lefthander, Steve Carlton, who was a match for the hard-throwing Lonborg. Boston scored only one unearned run in the six innings Carlton pitched, so throughout Lonborg had little margin for error. And he made none through eight innings, nipping the corners of the plate with an assortment of serves, all of them around knee-height, with an occasional brush-back pitch to assure Cardinal hitters that the inner tiger was still growling.

The only hits in eight innings off Lonborg were an infield single by Dal Maxvill in the third inning and a clean basehit to right by Roger Maris in the fourth. In the ninth, the Red Sox finally gave Jim some breathing room. Ron Willis was the pitcher now, Carlton having been removed for a pinch-hitter, and he walked George Scott. Reggie Smith, the rookie wonder, doubled into the left field corner, and Rico Petrocelli was walked intentionally. Here ex-Yankee Elston Howard came up and Willis was replaced by Jack Lamabe. Howard looked at a ball, swung at a strike and then blooped a single down the right field foul line, just beyond Maris's reach. Two runs scored and it gave Lonborg a 3–0 edge. The Cardinals were up for their last licks and the first two men, Brock and Flood, went out on routine grounders. But Roger Maris slammed a home run to end Lonborg's scoreless Series streak at seventeen innings.

The Red Sox were still alive, thanks to Lonborg. "Never do I remember . . . never . . . a more ecstatic, a more vigorous moment," he said later. Rookie manager Dick Williams beamed delightedly and said, "This may be the Year of Yastrzemski; this is the Day of Lonborg." Coach Sal Maglie shook his head appreciatively noting that Lonborg threw an even 100 pitches, two more than he used in his one-hitter. And catcher Elston Howard, around for thirteen years in the majors, termed Lonborg's performance as "one of the finest I've ever caught. I think he was better here than he was in the one-hit game in Boston." Lonborg agreed that this was his greatest game.

Boston won the next game in Fenway Park to tie the Series at 3–3, but in the finale Bob Gibson again was too much for the Red Sox and a fatigued Lonborg, pitching with two days rest. The Cardinals became world's champions.

But for Lonborg, and for millions of others, the greatest day was October 9, 1967, the day he brought the Red Sox from the dead.

THE BOX SCORE
(October 9, 1967)

BOSTON	A.B.	R.	H.	P.	A.		ST. LOUIS	A.B.	R.	H.	P.	A.
Foy, 3b.	5	1	1	2	4		Brock, lf.	4	0	0	0	0
Andrews, 2b.	3	0	1	1	2		Flood, cf.	4	0	2	0	0
Yastrze'ski, lf.	3	0	1	2	0		Maris, rf.	4	1	2	3	0
Harrelson, rf.	3	0	1	1	0		Cepeda, 1b.	4	0	0	5	0
Tartabull, rf.	0	0	0	0	0		McCarver, c.	3	0	0	9	1
Scott, 1b.	3	1	0	14	0		Shannon, 3b.	3	0	1	1	3
Smith, cf.	4	1	1	1	0		Javier, 2b.	3	0	0	4	3
Petrocelli, ss.	3	0	0	1	2		Maxvill, ss.	2	0	1	3	4
Howard, c.	4	0	1	5	0		bRicketts	1	0	0	0	0
Lonborg, p.	4	0	0	0	2		Willis, p.	0	0	0	0	0
							Lamabe, p.	0	0	0	0	1
							Carlton, p.	1	0	0	0	0
							aTolan	1	0	0	0	0
							Washburn, p.	0	0	0	0	1
							cGagliano	1	0	0	0	0
							Bressoud, ss.	0	0	0	0	0
Totals	32	3	6	27	10		Totals	31	1	3	27	13

BOSTON	0	0	1	0	0	0	0	0	2—3
ST. LOUIS	0	0	0	0	0	0	0	0	1—1

BOSTON	IP.	H.	R.	ER.		ST. LOUIS	IP.	H.	R.	ER.
Lonborg (W.)	9	3	1	1		Carlton (L.)	6	3	1	0
						Washburn	2	1	0	0
						Willis	0*	1	2	1
						Lamabe	1	1	0	0

*Pitched to three batters in ninth.

Bases on balls—Off Carlton 2 (Yastrzemski, Harrelson), off Willis 2 (Scott, Petrocelli). Struck out—By Lonborg 4 (Cepeda, Brock, Shannon, Tolan), by Carlton 5 (Foy, Scott, Lonborg 2, Yastrzemski), by Washburn 2 (Petrocelli, Foy), by Lamabe 2 (Lonborg, Foy). aStruck out for Carlton in sixth. bGrounded out for Maxvill in eighth. cPopped out for Washburn in eighth. Runs batted in—Harrelson, Howard, Maris. Two-base hits—Maris. Sacrifice hit—Andrews. Double plays—Javier, Maxvill and Cepeda; McCarver, Javier, McCarver, Shannon. Lamabe and McCarver. Wild pitch—Carlton. Left on bases—Boston 7, St. Louis 3. Umpires—Runge (AL) plate, Pryor (NL) first base, Stevens (AL) second base, Barlick (NL) third base, Umont (AL) left field, Donatelli (NL) right field. Time—2:20. Attendance—54,575.

MICKEY MANTLE

as told to Dan Daniel

Mickey Mantle (named after Hall of Famer, Mickey Cochrane) was born at Spavinaw, Olkahoma, October 20, 1931, came up with the Yankees in the spring of 1951 at age 19, and has remained to become one of the superstars of this, or any other, era. He is one of seven sluggers to crash 400 or more homers in his career. He was the Most Valuable of the Yankees in the last decade, topping such performers as Whitey Ford, Yogi Berra, Gil McDougald and Roger Maris. The $1,200 given him by super-scout Tom Greenwade to sign with the Yankee organization remains one of the all-time bargains. Mickey has two brothers who played briefly in the lower echelons of the Yankee farm system.

In 1967 Mantle became the sixth player in major league history to hit more than 500 home runs. To help preserve his distressed knees, the Yankees made him a first baseman, a position he played creditably.

For a ball player with batting aspirations, the day that stands out in his recollection is the one that saw him hit his first home run in the major leagues.

For me, that day was Tuesday, May 1, 1951, and the scene was Comiskey Park in Chicago.

We were opening our first invasion of the West. The White Sox had given some evidences of the great form with which they were to run up 14 straight victories, and establish themselves in first place.

It was a hot, sunny afternoon. We had played a dozen games, and I had done little to justify Casey Stengel's having kept me, instead of shipping me to Kansas City, or back with Harry Craft, my manager at Independence and Joplin, who was running the Yankee farm at Beaumont.

In fact, as we faced lefthander Bob Cain in that game at Comiskey Park, my batting average had dropped to a shabby .222, and there had been stories in the New York sports pages about Casey's plan to bench me against lefthanders, and make a lefthanded batter out of me, exclusively.

The experts had dug up the fact that against lefthanded pitching my average was something like .150.

However, on the trip from New York to Chicago, Stengel changed his mind. He kept me in the lineup against Cain and that gave me a terrific lift. Within a week I was up at the .303 level.

In any event, as we opened at Comiskey Park I felt that my first American League home run was long overdue. I had hit eight during the training season, and had led the writers to believe that I might continue that pace for the Yankees.

Well, game followed game, and those pitchers showed me tricks I never knew men could do with a baseball.

They pulled the string when I figured they would fast ball me. They threw speed when I expected soft stuff. They hurled sinkers and sliders, screwballs and knucklers, curves and fast balls, in a bewildering style that really had me dazed.

However, I knew I could hit, and I never lost my confidence. Sure, I got down. I was sore at myself, and I felt sorry for Stengel, who had gone out on a limb to give me my chance.

In my first appearance against Cain, who was to shut us out later in the season, after the Yankees had played 109 games without having been prevented from scoring, I lifted a fly to second baseman Nelson Fox.

In the second inning, I got on base through an error by third sacker Orestes Minoso and in the fourth I drove in a run with a long fly to center fielder Jimmy Busby.

In the fifth inning, Yogi Berra got to Cain for a homer. That gave me notions. But Cain wasn't to pitch to me again that afternoon.

When I came to bat in the sixth, Vic Raschi was on second with one out, and righthander Randy Gumpert, former Yankee, was the Chicago pitcher.

His first delivery to me was a fast ball, just right. I drove it into the right center seats, just off the center field bleachers. The press box called it a 440 foot drive. It went on a line. My first homer in the majors.

There was a small delegation of service men, guests of the Chicago club, where my thrill hit landed. One of those soldiers got the ball. He was a pleasant faced Negro lad.

I wanted that ball and asked Arthur E. (Red) Patterson, public relations man of the Yankees, to go after it.

Red chased out to that right center pavilion and offered the GI five dollars for the ball. He gave Patterson a big smile, and a very definite "No, nothing doin'."

Patterson is one of those men who do not give up. He kept after the soldier, and finally the GI hollered, "Man, what I want most right now is for you to let me alone. I will pay you $5 to bother me no more."

Finally even the persistent Red had to admit defeat. But he still did not give up. He went down into the Yankee bullpen, just under the soldier's seat and told catcher Ralph Houk to get that ball for me.

Houk went to work on the soldier in a gentle way. He impressed on him the fact that I was just a rookie, that I wanted that ball more than anything else in the world, and what a shame it would be if I had to leave the park without this souvenir of my first batting feat in the American League.

Charley Silvera, who was in the bullpen with Houk, said that night, "I never knew Ralph could operate so neatly as a persuader. He had all of us out there close to tears. The GI got so sentimental, he forgot to ask for the five that Patterson wanted to give him for the ball."

The Major delivered the ball to me in the clubhouse after we had beaten the White Sox by 8 to 3. I lost no time shipping the ball to Miss Merlyn Johnson, Picher, Okla.

I had a much bigger day against the White Sox in the Stadium on June 19, when we split a doubleheader with them. I hit a home run in each game, got four hits for ten bases, drove in four runs, stole a base, took a walk, but— went out on strikes twice.

In the first game, I drove a three and two pitch off Lou Kretlow into the right center bleachers with two on. I got two singles later on in that contest, which we won by 11 to 9.

In the nightcap, won by Chicago, 5 to 4, I got to Joe Dobson for my sixth home run with the Yankees.

It was a very satisfying drive because it brought my runs driven in total to 42, and helped me to maintain the club leadership in that detail, which they tell me is very important.

At the close of this big day, one of the New York writers told me that I had made 14 hits, three of them homers, as many more doubles, and one triple, against Chicago pitching in nine games, and was going at a .389 clip in competition with Paul Richards' hurlers.

May 1, which brought my first big league homer, was my day of days. But I got just as big a thrill on the morning of May 17.

As you know, all major league clubs have to get down to the 25 player limit within 30 days after the opening of the season. May 16 was cutting down day, and as it dawned, I was batting .301 and had driven in 21 runs, but I still wasn't sure that I would survive the pruning of the roster. The Yankees were quite a few over the limit, and I figured I might get a ticket to Kansas City.

A lot of us, on all sixteen clubs in the major leagues, were afraid that day. Some were to suffer similar fears through June 15, the trading deadline.

Anyway, on the 16th of May I got my third homer, against Dick Rozek, of Cleveland, in the Stadium, lifting my average to .308 in an 11 to 3 victory. I also got a single and a pass and stole a base. But if I had been ticketed for Kansas City, my achievements that afternoon would not have saved me.

I got up very early the next morning and scanned the sports pages. Mickey Mantle still was with the Yankees, and still had that No. 6 locker in the Yankee clubhouse, and I am not ashamed to admit that Mantle cried for joy.

The emergence of Mickey Mantle as a star of the first magnitude on the heels of Joe DiMaggio's retirement has enabled the Yankees to offer an unbroken lure at the box office for almost three decades, a source of envy to all other major league clubs. Mantle, although beset by injuries, has managed to rise above them, has been a member of ten championship clubs, and was the League's Most Valuable player in 1956, 1957, and 1962.

In 1956 he won the coveted "Triple Crown," indicating supremacy in batting average (.353), homers (52), and runs batted in (130). Only a half-dozen others have accomplished this feat.

Mantle now lives in Dallas, is involved in a wide variety of ventures, has become a proficient golfer. His chief complaint is that Mickey Jr. shows a lack of interest in the weekly batting averages.

JUAN MARICHAL

as told by Jack Orr

Juan Antonio (Sanchez) Marichal, whose hallmark is the highest leg-kick delivery baseball has seen in a generation, was born October 30, 1937, at Laguna Verde, Montecristi, Dominican Republic. He spent only two years in the minors before splashing upon the big league scene with the San Francisco Giants in 1960. Despite a series of crippling injuries (a pulled hamstring muscle, a spiked foot, a fractured hand and innumerable sore arms), he became a remarkably consistent winner, twice chalking up 25 in a season. At the end of seven seasons he had won 144 games to 68 defeats, a .679 percentage, a mark topped by only one man (Lefty Grove) installed in baseball's Hall of Fame at Cooperstown, New York, a destination Juan is almost certain to reach after his retirement. At that time, too, he will probably return to the Dominican Republic, where he already is among the richest farmland owners, purchases made possible by the $100,000 annual salary he made with the Giants.

MOST NATIONAL League hitters will agree that Juan Marichal was the most overpowering hurler the league had in the 1960s. One of his secrets is almost unbelievable control and his pitches almost always blaze in knee-high and away to the hitter whether Juan comes straight overhead, three-quarter or sidearm. His pinpoint control is evidenced by his

1,417 strikeouts, opposed to 343 bases on balls, a ratio of four and a half strikeouts to every walk he issued. As a point of comparison, Sandy Koufax, in eleven years, had a strikeout-walk ratio of barely over three to one.

Ironically, it was lack of control of a different sort which many observers believe cost Marichal the honor of becoming the first 30-game National League winner since Dizzy Dean's 1934 performance. That lack-of-control game was the infamous display at Candlestick Park, San Francisco, August 22, 1965, against Los Angeles. The Dodgers and Giants were, as usual, in the thick of a pennant fight and there had been a number of near-incidents and dugout insults as the key series rolled on. The pitchers were Marichal and Koufax and the 42,283 fans could feel the tension in the air. Both of these fine pitchers appeared to be throwing bullets not toward the plate but toward the batter.

Now it was the third inning, with Marichal at bat and the Giants trailing, 2–0. Koufax let loose a pitch that slithered through catcher John Roseboro's glove and rolled a few feet behind the plate. Roseboro retrieved the ball and threw it swiftly back to Koufax, the ball whizzing close to Marichal's head. Juan spun around and said hotly, "You better not hit me with that ball." Roseboro answered with some unprintable remarks. Then the two men confronted each other and the bubbling anger, the heat of the pennant race, the simmering situation all exploded at once. Marichal axed Roseboro with his bat, splitting open his skull. Roseboro tried blindly to get at his foe. Players spilled out of dugouts. For a moment it looked as if a riot were to break out. But peacemaking efforts by Koufax of the Dodgers and Willie Mays, springing out of the dugout, calmed the atmosphere. Marichal was ejected from the game, and Roseboro couldn't continue because of his injury. National League president Warren Giles slapped a nine-day suspesion on Marichal and fined him $1,750. In the game itself, the Giants went on to beat Koufax on Willie Mays' three-run homer.

The incident seemed to break Marichal's stride, for he lost four more games, in addition to the three starts the suspension cost him. He wound up 22–13, one of his four 20-victory seasons, and the following year, 1966, he was back on the beam with his best season to date, 25–6. The Giants lost the pennant, however, and many observers believe that if the beating incident had not occurred, the San Francisco entry would have been pennant-winner, instead of the Dodgers.

That was the year Marichal pitched 10 shutouts to lead the league, but he didn't seem to be the same after the Roseboro fracas. Still, he returned in 1966 with his best record yet, 25–6, and he kept San Francisco in the pennant race until the final 24 hours of the season. He again was the overpowering master he had been in 1962, 1963 and 1964. In one season over that span he pitched 321⅓ innings, surpassing Carl Hubbell's 313 in 1934. It was a durability achievement unsurpassed by a Giant pitcher in sixty years.

And 1963 marked several other high spots. He pitched his one and only no-hit game against the Houston Colt .45s in June of that year, and he tangled with the brilliant Warren Spahn of the Braves in a 16-inning beauty which then manager Alvin Dark called "the greatest pitching duel I ever saw."

In the no-hitter, Juan faced only 29 men, walking Al Spangler and Bob Aspromonte, but it wasn't an easy task. The Giants failed to get him a run until the eight when Jim Davenport and Chuck Hiller doubled. The score was 1–0.

In the sixteen-inning game at Candlestick Park, Spahn pitched superb ball himself, throwing only 200 pitches. But one of them was a homer by Willie Mays in the bottom of the sixteenth and that was another game to write the folks back in Monte Criste about.

Reviewing his seven years in the majors, Marichal likes to recall his 25th victory in 31 decisions in the nerve-racking pennant race of 1966. And for once, the game wasn't against the arch rival Los Angeles club, though that team was definitely involved in the final two days of the season.

On the Saturday before the season closed, the Giants were nipping at the Dodgers' heels. Los Angeles, by virtue of a splendid September run, held the slimmest of leads. By Saturday night, the Giants had won a doubleheader from the Pirates and the Dodgers had been rained out in Philadelphia and a doubleheader had been scheduled for the final Sunday. If Los Angeles lost its season-ending twin bill and the San Francisco club won its three games with the Pirates, another National League playoff would have been in the offing.

Marichal drew the first assignment to keep Giants hopes flickering. He was less than at his best, and Pittsburgh, too,

THE BOX SCORE
(October 1, 1966)

SAN FRANCISCO   PITTSBURGH

	A.B.	R.	H.	RBI.		A.B.	R.	H.	RBI.
Fuentes, ss.	4	0	1	0	M. Alou, cf.	5	1	1	0
J. Alou, lf.	3	0	0	0	Alley, ss.	5	0	1	0
McC'y, ph.-1b.	2	0	0	0	Mota, lf.	4	1	1	0
Mays, cf.	4	0	0	0	Clemente, rf.	3	2	3	2
Hart, 3b.	4	2	2	0	Clendenon, 1b.	4	0	2	2
Hiatt, 1b.	3	1	2	1	Mazeroski, 2b.	4	0	1	0
Gabrielson, lf.	0	0	0	0	Bailey, 3b.	3	0	3	0
Johnson, lf.	1	0	1	0	Pagan, 3b.	0	0	0	0
Brown, rf.	5	2	2	3	Stargell, ph.	1	0	0	0
Barton, c.	3	0	0	0	Michael, 3b.	0	0	0	0
Haller, ph.-c.	0	0	0	0	Gonder, c.	4	0	1	0
Lanier, 2b.	2	0	1	0	Fryman, p.	1	0	0	0
D'port, ph.-2b.	2	0	1	1	Blass, p.	0	0	0	0
Marichal, p.	3	0	1	0	Spriggs, ph.	1	0	0	0
					O'Dell, p.	1	0	0	0
					Mikkelsen, p.	0	0	0	0
					Law, p.	0	0	0	0
					Lynch, ph.	1	0	0	0
Totals	36	5	11	5	Totals	37	4	13	4

SAN FRANCISCO	0 0 0 3 0 0 0 2 0—5	
PITTSBURGH	0 1 0 0 3 0 0 0 0—4	

SAN FRANCISCO

	IP.	H.	R.	ER.	BB.	SO.
Marichal (W. 25-6)	9	13	4	4	1	3

PITTSBURGH

	IP.	H.	R.	ER.	BB.	SO.
Fryman	4*	4	3	3	2	4
Blass	1	0	0	0	0	0
O'Dell	1⅓	2	0	0	0	0
Mikkelsen (L. 9-8)	1	3	2	2	2	0
Law	1⅔	2	0	0	0	2

*Pitched to two batters in fifth.

E—Hiatt. DP—San Francisco 2. LOB—San Francisco 10, Pittsburgh 7. 2B—Brown, Celmente, Bailey. 3B—Hart. HR—Clemente (29), Brown (7). SH—Fuentes, Gabrielson. T—2:45.

was scrambling for part of the final action. All in all, Juan was touched for 13 hits, most of them singles. But he was a tough nut to crack with men on bases and the Bucs stranded 10 base runners as Marichal poured it on when he needed to. Still, even though he had a 3–1 advantage by the fifth, on hits by Jim Ray Hart and rookie Jack Hiatt and a homer by Ollie Brown, but that lead disappeared on hits by Donn Clendenon and Roberto Clemente, for a 4–3 Pirate lead.

But in the eighth Hart walked, was sacrificed to second and scored the tying run on Brown's double. Jim Davenport came through with another hit for the lead run. Then they handed the ball with the one-run lead on it to Marichal for the eighth and ninth innings. He blew down the Pirates with ease, getting six straight batsman and insuring his part in the critical drive.

The Giants won the second Saturday game and again on Sunday, so they still had a chance to tie for the flag if the Phillies managed to knock off the erstwhile Brooklyns. And the Phils did win the first game, 4–3. That left the Giants sitting around the Pittsburgh airport waiting for the outcome of the nightcap. Walter Alston, the Dodger skipper, did the only thing he could: he pitched Sandy Koufax out of turn and Sandy, though given a scare in the ninth when the Phils scored three times and had the winning runs on base, stiffened mightily to retire the next three hitters, two by strikeouts. In Pittsburgh, the Giants sighed and headed for their homes.

It was an occasion for gloom, but despite the sorrowful moment, the Giant players came up, one by one, to shake Marichal's hand. He had given them their opportunity for glory and the 1966 Series with his spectacular 25 victories, despite an injury that sidelined him for a month. And his final victory had kept them in contention until 7:15 p.m. on the October Sunday that marked the end of the race. He had given them his all, and his teammates wanted to show him they knew it.

ROGER MARIS

as told by Jack Orr

Thirty-four years after Babe Ruth's awesome 1927 season in which he hit 60 home runs, a complicated young man named Roger Maris hit 61. The exploit was not greeted with much enthusiasm by fans or sports writers, even those with New York Yankee persuasion. Expansion of the league had extended the season from 154 games to 162, and thus, it was charged, Maris's was tainted. He was booed roundly for five years before Yankee management gave up and traded him to the St. Louis Cardinals for a mediocre third baseman, Charlie Smith. The Card fans accepted Rog warmly, and instead of quitting the game as he had threatened, Maris responded by playing a key role in the Cards' domination of the baseball world in 1967. Still only 33 (he was born in Fargo, North Dakota, September 10, 1934), it is likely he will have a number of productive years in his warm new home.

UNTIL THE magic year of 1961, Roger Maris was a sound, less than explosive outfielder who could go a distance for a fly ball and who had a fine, accurate arm. In three years with Cleveland and Kansas City in the American League he had set no worlds afire. He averaged nineteen homers a year, drove in about seventy runs, but his batting averages were .235, .240 and .273.

Then he was traded from the Athletics to the Yankees in one of those blood relative deals those clubs used to pull off in the pre-Finley era, with Maris, first baseman Kent Hadley and shortstop Joe DeMaestri going to New York in exchange for Don Larsen, the perfect game pitcher, and Marv Throneberry, Hank Bauer and Norm Siebern. The change of climate at first acted wonders on Roger, though he was not happy in New York primarily because his wife and family continued to live in Independence, Missouri. But it didn't seem to affect his play. In his very first game as a Yankee, he hit two homers, a double and a single. Over the first half of the year he carried the team almost singlehandedly, then a rib injury took him out of action. The Yankees won the pennant anyway (Casey Stengel's last), but lost to the Pirates in the Series.

Despite his slump in the latter half of the season, Maris hit .283, his highest major league average. His 93 runs scored and his 39 home runs were second best in the league and he drove in 112 teammates. He was named the American League's Most Valuable Player. Casey Stengel agreed. "Let me tell you about him," he told a sports writer. "I give him one point for speed. I do this because he can run fast. I give him another point because he can slide fast. Then I give him a point because he can bunt. I also give him a point because he can field, very good around the fences, even on top of the fences. Next, I give him a point because he can throw. A right fielder has to be a thrower or he's not a right fielder. So I add up my points and I've got five for him before I even come to his hitting. I would say this is a good man."

The following year all anybody would talk about was his hitting—his homer hitting. He started slowly, getting only three homers in the first 27 games of the season. Then in the next 16 games he hit 12 homers and batted .300. In June he hit 15 more home runs to reach No. 34 and he had 40 by August 1.

That was about when the arguments about Ruth's sacrosanct record began developing. One argument ran that even if Maris did hit 60 or more (and he was already three weeks ahead of the Babe's schedule), he would have to do it in 154 games as Ruth did or it wouldn't count. Others countered by saying a record was a record and the details didn't matter. When the fiber glass pole was developed, every pole vault record in the books was broken a dozen times. The vaulters of the past may have been just as good as the present-day ones, but that did not change the fact that the seventeen-foot pole vault is accepted as the record. The counter argument ran that it would be terrible to have that priceless record broken by a combination of the modern-day lively ball and an extended season.

Finally, Ford C. Frick, then Commissioner of Baseball, ruled that Ruth's record would have to be broken in 154 games or less. Frick actually didn't say that an asterisk would accompany Maris's name in the record books if it took him more than 154 games, but, in effect, that was exactly what happened. If you look it up now, there are parentheses after Maris's 61 homers which say: "162-game season."

Maris did not consider himself a superstar. Even when he hit his 50th home run, off Ken McBride in Los Angeles, and became only the ninth player in history to hit that many in a season, he modestly put in a disclaimer.

"I never wanted all this hoopla. All I wanted is to be a good ball player, hit 25 or 30 homers, drive in around a hundred runs, hit .280 and help my club win pennants. I just wanted to be one of the guys, an average player having a good season."

Instead, the spotlight glared on him mercilessly. It glared particularly during the month of September, as he hit Nos. 52, 53, 54, 55 and 56. That last was on September 9, the 142d game of the year and it meant he had twelve games in which to hit five homers to smash the sacred mark. Every day at the ball park he was surrounded by dozens of reporters. Not a day passed without a newspaper, magazine or newsreel editor trying to get an exclusive interview at his apartment in Manhattan.

Everything he said or did or even thought was printed in the newspapers and Maris, always a blunt outspoken man, said just what he thought. The stories made the fans react against Maris, and he was less than a popular hero. He snapped back at fans and reporters and that led to further taunts and an even rougher press, which led to Maris snapping more sharply. He was under so much pressure that his hair literally began to fall out. His doctor told him it was pure nerves.

Amazingly, Maris continued to hit home runs. From the time in April when he hit one off Detroit's Paul Foytack until he arrived at game No. 154 in Baltimore's Memorial Stadium, he had deposited 58 over the fence. (Actually, he had hit 59 but he lost one earlier in Baltimore in July when a game was rained out before the clout could become official.) So going into this night game on September 20, he needed two home runs to equal Ruth's 154-game standard.

The first time up against Milt Pappas, a solid righthander of the Orioles, Maris slashed a hard drive to right field where it was caught. If it had been a couple of feet higher, it would have been out of reach and would have gone for homer No. 59. Maris *did* get his 59th on the next trip to the plate in the third inning, a four-hundred-foot drive to deep right field.

Now it was the fifth inning and the pitcher slipped two quick strikes past Rog. Then he hit another line drive deep to right field, but it curved just foul. Then he struck out. In the seventh, he hit another high fly deep to right, but again it went foul. With two strikes on him now, Maris swung again and his long fly was caught in deep right center. If he had pulled it more to the right it would have been a homer. If he had pulled it a little lower, a little more on a line, it would have carried over the fence. In the ninth, against Hoyt Wilhelm, the knucklballer, Maris pulled away from a pitch but the knockler bobbed and weaved and hit Roger's bat, rolled back to the pitcher, who threw him out.

"So he didn't hit his 60th that night," his teammate Mickey Mantle recalled, "but what a try he gave it. Even the best homer hitters average about nine or ten at-bats for every homer. That night, in five at-bats, Rog hit five long drives that could have been homers (and of course one was), and it was one of the greatest shows of power hitting I ever saw, coming at the absolute clutch moment. He didn't have much luck that night, but he had all the rest—skill and power and all the courage a man could want.

"Sure, Rog got two more after that to break the Babe's record, but I think those of us who played with the Yankees that year were even prouder of Roger that night in Baltimore than when he finally did go ahead of the Babe. We knew what he had been through all season and we knew the pressure that was on him that night. We knew how much he wanted No. 60 in that game, No. 154. I think the try he made, the courage he showed that night, meant more to us than all the homers he hit. Incidentally, that was the night the Yankees clinched the pennant on his 59th."

Maris got No. 60 off John Fisher of Baltimore in

the Yankee's 159th game of the season, and then hit his sixty-first at the Stadium off Tracy Stallard of the Red Sox in the last game of the year. In the fourth, with one out and nobody on, Maris faced Stallard and the Stadium crowd grew hushed. The first pitch was low and outside for a ball. The second was inside, another ball. The crowd began to boo Stallard.

Stallard's next pitch was a fast ball, waist high, straight down the middle. Maris uncoiled, flashing that graceful, fluid swing. He hit it well. The ball went soaring high and deep toward right field, and in the stands everybody was on his feet shouting, "Homer! Homer!" Fathers lifted their sons high into the air so the youngsters could see the ball land ten rows back and ten feet to the right of the Yankee bullpen.

Marris jogged around the bases, stonefaced, and quietly acknowledged the cheers. When he reached the dugout his teammates wouldn't let him enter until he went back out on the field and waved his hat to the hysterical crowd. "I was up there wheeling," Maris told the reporters around his

THE BOX SCORE
(October 1, 1961)

BOSTON (A.)	A.B.	R.	H.	RBI.	NEW YORK (A.)	A.B.	R.	H.	RBI.
Schilling, 2b.	4	0	1	0	Richards'n, 2b.	4	0	0	0
Geiger, cf.	4	0	0	0	Kubek, ss.	4	0	2	0
Yast'mski, lf.	4	0	1	0	Maris, cf.	4	1	1	0
Malzone, 3b.	4	0	0	0	Berra, lf.	2	0	0	0
Clinton, rf.	4	0	0	0	Lopez, lf.,-rf.	1	0	0	0
Runnels, 1b.	3	0	0	0	Blanchard, rf.-c.	3	0	0	0
Gile, 1b.	0	0	0	0	Howard, c.	2	0	0	0
Nixon, c.	3	0	2	0	Reed, lf.	1	0	1	0
Green, ss.	2	0	0	0	Skowron, 1b.	2	0	0	0
Stallard, p.	1	0	0	0	Hale, 1b.	1	0	1	0
bJensen	1	0	0	0	Boyer, 3b.	2	0	0	0
Nichols, p.	0	0	0	0	Stafford, p.	2	0	0	0
					Reniff, p.	0	0	0	0
					aTresh	1	0	0	0
					Arroyo, p.	0	0	0	0
Totals	30	0	4	0	Totals	29	1	5	1

aPopped up for Reniff in 7th; bPopped up for Stallard in 8th.

```
BOSTON     0 0 0 0 0 0 0 0 0—0
NEW YORK   0 0 0 1 0 0 0 0 x—1
```

E—None. LOB—Boston 5, New York 5.

locker. "Yes, I'm happy about it all, happy it's all over. Now I hope I can just be back to being a regular ball player."

But in subsequent years the fans wouldn't let him play that role. He hit only 33 homers the next year, 23 the year after than, and then 26, 8 and 13. Injured a good deal of the time, he sometimes appeared as if he weren't really trying. So in a desperation move after the 1966 season, when the Yankees plunged into the league cellar, the club unloaded Maris to the Cardinals and he became a happy and formidable performer for the National Leaguers. He drove in more runs than anyone in the 1967 World Series (7), won at least one ball game with a timely hit, smacked a homer and was a rock in right field as the Cardinals became World's Champions.

Still, it is unlikely that he will ever forget to tell his children of his fabled 1961 season when he hit 61 home runs—more than anyone in the history of the game.

CHRISTY MATHEWSON

as told by Lloyd Lewis

*One of the first college graduates in the hurly-burly era
of baseball, Christopher "Big Six" Mathewson, born
August 12, 1880, in Factoryville, Pennsylvania, was
also the first of its great pitchers. Christy was with the
New York Giants from 1900 through 1916, moving on
to Cincinnati as manager of the Reds in 1917. In 17
active seasons, Matty won 373 games and compiled the
highest lifetime pitching percentage of any National
League pitcher. A victim of tuberculosis, while in the
prime of life, Matty died on October 7, 1925.*

WHEN THE bleacher gates at Shibe Park in Philadelphia were
thrown open on the morning of October 24, 1911, I was in
the mob that went whooping toward the front seats. I got
one, partly because the right-field crowd was smaller than the
one in left. Most Philadelphians wanted to sit close to their
worshiped Athletics, for the World Series at that moment
stood two games to one for Connie Mack against John Mc-
Graw, and Philadelphia was loud and passionate in the confidence that now they would get revenge for the bitter dose
—4 games to 1—three shutouts the Giants had given them
six years before.

Me, I wanted to get as close to the Giants as possible, and
found a place at the rail close to the empty chairs which
would that afternoon become the Giants' bull pen. My whole
adolescence had been devoted, so far as baseball went—and
it went a long way to an Indiana farm boy—to the Giants and

113

to their kingly pitcher, the great, the incomparable Christy Mathewson. I hadn't had the courage to cut classes in the nearby college and go to the first game of the Series at Shibe Park. But today I had. Things were desperate. Up in New York's Polo Grounds to start this, the World Series, Mathewson had won—2 to 1—giving but five hits and demonstrating that with 12 years of herculean toil behind him he was practically as invincible as when in 1905 he had shut out these same Athletics three times.

It had looked like 1905 over again; then in the second game, the A's long, lean yokel third baseman J. Franklin Baker had suddenly and incredibly knocked a home run off Rube Marquard, the Giants' amazing young pitcher. Baker, who had hit only 9 homers all season, had tagged the 22-year-old Giant and two runs had come in—and the final score had stood 3-1.

The papers which I read, as the morning wore on, were still full of that home run and its aftermath.

From the start of the series the newspapers had been publishing syndicated articles signed by Giant and Athletic stars ——the real start of the "ghost writers" whose spurious trade flourished so long but which the better papers in time eliminated. And in the article signed by Mathewson the day after Marquard's disaster it had been said that Rube had lost the game by failing to obey orders. The article rebuked the boy for throwing Baker the high outside pitch he liked, instead of the low fast one he didn't like and which McGraw had ordered.

The rebuke had been a sensation which grew in the third game when Baker had hit another homer off Mathewson himself, and had been the main wrecker of the great man's long sway over the A's. Up to the ninth inning of that third game Matty had kept command. Always when the Athletics had got men on bases he had turned on his magic. As he went to the bench at the end of the eighth, New York had risen and given him a tremendous ovation, for in 44 innings of World Series play, 1905 and 1911, he had allowed the Mackmen exactly one run—and the A's were hitters, indeed. Their season's average for 1911 had been .297.

Then in the ninth, Eddie Collins had gone out, and only two men had stood between Matty and his fifth series victory over his victims. Up had come Baker with the American

League fans begging him to do to Matty what he had done to Marquard—and, incredible as it seemed, he did.

As home runs go, it hadn't been much more than a long fly that sailed into the convenient right-field stand at the Polo Grounds, but it went far enough to tie the score and give Baker a nickname for life—"Home Run" Baker.

Snodgrass, the Giants' center fielder, one of the smartest and greatest of base runners, had ripped Baker's trousers almost off him, sliding into third in the first of the 10th inning. With McGraw snarling, railing, jeering from the coaching line, the Giants made no secret of their hatred of Baker. To them he was merely a lucky lout, a greenhorn who had by sheer accident homered off the two top pitchers of the season.

But Baker had hit again, a scratch single in the eleventh which had been part of the making of the run which had won, and Marquard in his "ghosted" article had quipped at Mathewson's advice.

All that was in everybody's mind—and mine, as on October 24 the fourth game came up. The papers had had time to chew the sensation over and over, for it had rained for a week after the third game and now, with seven days' rest, Mathewson was to try again—this time in Shibe Park.

The long delay hadn't cooled excitement. The press box was still as crowded as at the opening game. This was the first World Series to be handled in the modern publicity fashion —the first to have as many as 50 telegraphers on the job—the first to wire the game play-by-play to points as distant as Havana, Cuba—the first to which newspapers in the Far West and South sent their own writers. And though the A's now had a lead of two games to one, the threat of the Giants was still great enough to keep fever high.

It was a little after 1 o'clock when my long vigil ended. Onto the field came the Giants with their immemorial swagger, chips still on their shoulders—the cocky, ornery, defiant men of Muggsy McGraw—the rip-roaring demons who had that season of 1911 set a record of 347 stolen bases—a record which would stand for another 31 years without any other club ever coming nearer to it than the Senators' 288 in 1913.

And here at long last they were. I knew them from their pictures as, clad in dangerous black, they came strutting across toward their dugout. McGraw had dressed his men in black, back in 1905 when he had humbled the Athletics, and he was playing hunches now.

Muggsy was first—stocky, hard-eyed. Behind him came slim, handsome Snodgrass, the great base-stealer who was a genius at getting hit by pitched balls and in scaring infielders with his flashing spikes. Then came swart, ominous Larry Doyle; lantern-jawed Art Fletcher; Buck Herzog, whose nose curved like a scimitar; lithe little Josh Devore; burly Otis Crandall; flat-faced mahogany-colored Chief Meyers, the full-blooded Indian; Fred Merkle, all muscles even in his jaws, a lion-heart living down the most awful bonehead blunder ever made in baseball.

Then came Marquard, 6 feet 3, his sharp face wreathed in a smile—his head tilting to the left at the top of a long wiry neck—Marquard the meteoric. At 19 years of age he had been bought at a record price from Indianapolis and had immediately flopped two straight years for McGraw, becoming the nationally goatish "$11,000 lemon." Then this 1911, he had flamed out, won 24 games and become the "$11,000 beauty."

As the Giants began to toss the ball around, I couldn't see my hero, the Mathewson whom I had come to see, the great one who from the time I was 9 I had pretended I was, playing ball in the Indiana cow pasture, throwing his famous "fade-away" which, for me, never came off. Then, suddenly, there he was, warming up and growling "Who am I working for, the Giants or the photographers," as the cameramen, not 20 feet from my popeyed head, begged him for poses.

I was let down for a minute. He didn't speak like a demi-god, but as I stared, he looked it, all the same. He held his head high, and his eye with slow, lordly contempt swept the Athletics as they warmed up across the field. He was 31, all bone and muscle and princely poise. Surely he would get those Athletics today and put the Giants back in the running. Surely his unique "fadeaway," the curve, his fabulous brain couldn't be stopped. It had been luck that had beaten him in the last game. Now he'd get them.

My eye never left him till the bell rang and he strode, hard but easy, with the swing of the aristocrat, into the dugout and little Josh Devore went up to hit.

Josh singled, Doyle tripled, Snodgrass scored Larry with a long fly. Black figures were flying everywhere. The big copper-colored Chief Bender on Mack's mound was wobbling, and when the side was finally out he practically ran for the dugout. Later, we learned, he had run in to cut out bandages from his ribs, from an old injury. After that he was to be unworkable.

Up came the Athletics. Matty, as though in princely disdain, fanned the first two men. The third man, Eddie Collins, singled. Here came Baker, his sun-tanned face tense, his bat flailing—the air thick with one word from 25,000 throats, "Homer! Homer!"

Matty studied him as a scientist contemplates a beetle, then struck him out! What I yelled, I don't know. All I remember is standing there bellowing and paying no heed to the wadded newspapers the Athletic fans around me threw. It was wonderful.

On the fourth, Baker came up to start it and doubled. Dannie Murphy doubled, Harry Davis doubled. Ira Thomas hit a sacrifice fly—three runs. It couldn't be. Up came Baker again in the fifth with Collins on first and another double boomed across the diamond. I saw Snodgrass eventually stop it, but he didn't really have it in his glove at all. It had stuck in my gullet.

Right in front of me an unthinkable thing happened. Hooks Wiltse, the southpaw, began warming up for the Giants. Was Matty knocked out? Another figure rose from the bull pen. Rube Marquard. He didn't warm up, he only strolled up and down, a great sardonic grin on his face. The fans around me were screaming at him, "You're even with Matty now, Rube! He won't tell you what to pitch anymore!" etc., etc. Rube smirked at them.

Matty got by without more scores, but in the seventh with a man on third Christy walked Baker and Shibe Park's walls waved in a cyclone of "boos." I wished I was dead.

The eighth. A pinch hitter went up for Mathewson. I was sorry I hadn't died in the seventh. Finally it was all over.

I walked out through 25,000 of the most loathsome individuals ever created—all peering at Mathewson, all howling Baker's virtues. I dragged my feet this way and that trying to escape the currents of fans. At the end of a dolorous mile I stopped at a saloon. I had never had a drink. Now was the time.

"Beer," I said, in the voice of Poe's raven.

"You ain't 21," the bartender rasped. Then he took a second look, saw that I was 100 years old, and splashed a great stein in front of me.

I took one swallow. It was bitter, just as bitter as everything else in the world. I laid down a nickel and walked out. Every step of the way downtown I kept telling myself that in my coffin, some day, there'd be only room for one thing besides myself—my hatred of the Athletics.

But what I started out to tell was about my greatest day in baseball. That came three years later, October 9, 1914, when the lowly despised Boston Braves wallowed, humbled, trampled, laughed at the lofty Athletics to the tune of 7 to 1. I came out of Shibe Park, spent hours hunting that same saloon, but I couldn't find it. It had to be that one. What I wanted to do was to walk in all alone—find nobody else in there—order two beers and when the bartender looked inquiringly at the extra one, say to him in a condescending voice, "Oh, that? That's for Mathewson."

WILLIE MAYS

as told by Jack Orr

Willie Mays was born on May 6, 1931, in a suburb of Birmingham, Alabama, called Westfield. At 18 he worked in a steel mill, and at 19 he was the most exciting rookie the game ever hatched. Over the years his greatness never dimmed. The late Branch Rickey, who had seen them all over a 60-year stretch, marveled at the intensity Mays brought to every hit, run and throw. Leonard Koppett, the knowledgeable New York Times senior baseball writer, said simply, "Mays is the greatest player I ever saw." One of Willie's biographers noted: "He is the most exciting of all players." Now 36 and nearing the end of almost two decades of electric play, he continues to be a Giant in every sense of the word.

For a glittering superstar of the durability and prowess of a Willie Mays it is nearly impossible for anyone to agree on the most exciting day in a career of scores of exciting days. Willie himself isn't quite sure which day he would choose. His idolaters in the bleachers and the press box are widely split.

Those who lean to the record book point to August 17, 1966, when under extreme pressure he clouted an historic homer off Ray Washburn of the Cardinals. It happened to be No. 535 of Willie's career, breaking Jimmy Foxx's lifetime mark of 534 and making Mays second only to the mighty Babe Ruth in total homers. Earlier that year he slammed his 512th home run, off the Dodgers' Claude Osteen, to break Mel Ott's all-time National League record. That was in Candlestick Park on May 4, and as soon as the ball was hit, the 28,220 fans rose to their feet and screamed joyously for more than fifteen minutes.

Others like to remember April 30, 1961, when to the astonishment of 13,114 citizens at Milwaukee's County Stadium, Mays hit four home runs in one game, undoubtedly his strongest day at the plate. He hit one off Lew Burdette in the first, nobody on; a second off Burdette in the third, one on; another off Seth Morehead in the sixth, two on, and another off Don McMahon in the eigth, one on. So, in all that day, Mays drove in eight runs. In his fifth time at bat he hit a line shot to dead centerfield off Moe Drabowsky, and had Willie got some loft to the ball, it would have meant five homers. It was only the ninth time in history that anyone had hit four in a single game. The others were Bobby Lowe, Ed Delahanty before the turn of the century, Lou Gehrig, Chuck Klein, Pat Seerey, Gil Hodges, Joe Adcock and Rocky Colavito in this century (and Klein and Seerey got theirs in extra-inning games). When one compares the feat with the 160 or so no-hitters, the staggering magnitude of Willie's day can be seen.

Then there were those days in the tail end of the 1962 season. The Giants had trailed the Dodgers most of the way and were still behind by a full game on the last day of the season. The Giants were playing Houston in San Francisco and the Dodgers were meeting the Cardinals in Los Angeles. For a season tie to ensue, the Giants had to win and the Dodgers had to lose, highly improbable at that stage of the game. But in the eighth inning of a 1–1 game in San Francisco, Willie timed a Dick Farrell fast ball and belted it far over the left field fence. The Giants won, 2–1. That doubled the pressure on the Dodgers, who were also in a tied-up game, 0–0, and when the Cards' Gene Oliver hit a homer off John Podres, the Dodgers lost and the flag race was forced into a playoff. That could have been Willie's greatest day, too.

The Giants lost the second playoff game, so it all came down to the 165th game of the 1962 season. In the ninth, trailing, 4–2, the Giants rallied and put two men in scoring position with Mays at bat. Dodger Ed Roebuck pitched carefully, but Willie almost tore the pitcher's hand off with a vicious drive that scored a run and set up the two runs which were to follow. Though a fly ball by Orlanda Cepeda brought in the tying run and a walk to Jim Davenport scored the run that was to be the winning one, most press hands agreed that it was Mays' ball game. "You knew," one writer said in his story, "that Mays had hammered the final nail, slammed the final lid, turned off the lights." Another memorable moment.

And then there were the golden days when Mays saved ball games with his superlative play in the field. Collectors of Maysabilia can't agree on which was the greatest of these, either. Giant vice-president Chub Feeney, who has seen all the catches Willie had made in his sixteen years in the majors, chooses one made in Chavez Ravine in 1964. "He was playing Tommy Davis away over in left-center," Feeney recalled, "but Davis smashed one to right-center. The ball was curving away from Willie, but he poured on the coal, leaped as high as he could, shot his left arm and gloved the ball. What he got his glove on was a three-base hit, spelled o-u-t." Another Giant camp follower, broadcaster Russ Hodges, voted for a play on Bobby Morgan at Ebbets Field in 1951 when the Dodgers were still in Brooklyn. There were two out, bases loaded, last of the ninth. Morgan's ball was hit to left center. All of a sudden it caught up with Willie, who dove for it knee-high. His left arm hit him in the stomach as he fell and it knocked him cold. But when he came to, the ball was still in his glove.

Then there was the remarkable event in the 1954 World Series when the Giants swept the Cleveland Indians in four straight games. Mays had a creditable hitting Series, but the year is remembered by most fans as the one of The Catch.

It came about in the opening game at New York's Polo Grounds. It was the top of the eighth inning in a bitterly, painfully slowly played ball game, score 2–2, none out. A base hit by Al Rosen off Al Darks' bare right hand had just driven Sal Maglie from the mound and sent Larry Doby to second. Don Liddle came in to pitch, a left-handed curveballer to work on left-handed hitting Vic Wertz. Liddle's curve hung high over the plate—and Wertz walloped it. The ball went on a high screaming line to dead centerfield. Mays turned full around, head down and ran as hard as he could straight toward the runway between the two bleacher sections. The ball raced him to the wall. Mays didn't leap for the ball. He just outran it, and at the last split second—just as it seemed the smash was going to carom off the grating at the foot of the bleachers—Willie put his hands high in front of his left shoulder like a large receptacle and caught the ball as a football end catches a leading pass in the end zone.

And Willie wasn't through. Even though he was running at top speed, away from the diamond, nearly 450 feet from home plate, he was able to whirl in front of the screen, head twisting to his left as his right arm swept around (his cap, inevitably, falling off), and he was able to fire a throw to Davey Williams standing at second base. Doby took third after the catch, but Rosen, shaken, scampered back to first. Mays had broken the back of the Indian attack—and when the Giants won in the tenth on a homer by Dusty Rhodes, the Indians were helpless tabby cats in the next three games.

Still, for the greatest day ever for Willie Howard Mays, you have to go all the way back to his rookie season in 1951. That was the year the Giants made their miraculous comeback in the last six weeks of the season to tie the Dodgers, who had led by 13½ games in mid-August, and defeat them in the dramatic third game of the playoff on Bobby Thomson's homer in the ninth—the shot that was heard from Maine to California. Beginning on August 12 the Giants went on a 16-game winning streak, nearly every game a heart-clutcher. You can see the scores—3–2, 2–1, 5–2, 4–2, 3–1, 2–1, 8–5, 2–0, 5–4, 7–4, 4–3, 6–5, 5–4, 5–1, 5–4 and 6–3—that each game was tight and Willie had a hand in most of the victories.

And the one play that may have turned around the whole year for both teams came on August 15. The Giants' streak had just about started—four in a row—and they were playing Brooklyn at the Polo Grounds. It was a 1–1 ball game, eighth inning, one out, Billy Cox on third, Ralph Branca on first and Carl Furillo up. In the stands there were 21,007 fidgety fans.

Furillo hit a fly ball into right center field. Mays, playing over in left-center for the notorious pull-hitting Furillo, had to come a long distance to make the catch. Make it he did, on the dead run, gloved hand extended, and that was the second out. But Cox on third had tagged up and was heading home with the lead run. And Cox could run like a deer. When Mays caught the fly ball, running full speed toward the right field foul line, he was moving away from the play. If he stopped dead and threw, he couldn't possibly

THE BOX SCORE
(August 15, 1951)

BROOKLYN (N.)	A.B.	R.	H.	P.	A.	NEW YORK (N.)	A.B.	R.	H.	P.	A.
Furillo, rf.	4	0	1	5	0	Stanky, 2b.	3	0	1	1	3
Reese, ss.	4	1	1	1	2	Dark, ss.	4	1	1	1	1
Snider, cf.	4	0	0	2	0	Mueller, rf.	3	0	0	2	0
Pafko, lf.	4	0	0	1	0	Irvin, lf.	3	0	1	2	0
Campan'la, c.	3	0	1	5	0	Lockman, 1b.	3	0	0	10	0
Hodges, 1b.	3	0	0	8	0	Mays, cf.	3	1	1	3	1
Cox, 3b.	3	0	2	1	1	Thomson, 3b.	3	0	0	1	3
Terw'l'ger, 2b.	2	0	0	1	3	Westrum, c.	3	1	1	7	1
Robinson, 2b.	1	0	0	0	0	Hearn, p.	3	0	0	0	2
Branca, p.	3	0	1	0	2						
Totals	31	1	6	24	8	Totals	28	3	5	27	11

BROOKLYN	0	0	0	0	0	0	1	0	0—1
NEW YORK	1	0	0	0	0	0	0	2	x—3

Runs batted in—Irvin, Campanella, Westrum 2.

Two-base hit—Dark. Home run—Westrum. Double plays—Branca, Reese and Hodges; Mays and Westrum. Left on bases—Brooklyn 3, New York 2. Bases on balls—Off Branca 1. Struck out—By Branca 5, Hearn 5. Wild pitch—Hearn. Balk—Hearn. Winning pitcher—Hearn (11-7). Losing pitcher—Branca (10-4). Umpires—Warneke, Goetz, Jorda and Dascoli. Time of game—2:10. Attendance—21,007.

get any zip on the ball. So he improvised. He caught the ball, planted his left foot and pivoted away from the plate, so that he threw like a discus thrower. Fans in the bleachers must have wondered what in the world their boy was doing.

The throw came to the plate as a bullet and Whitey Lockman, the cut-off man, let it go through and Wes Westrum, the catcher, caught it belt-high and slapped a tag on a desperately sliding Cox. "For a long time," a reporter said in his paper the next day, "the stands were silent, not quite certain they had seen right. Then they exploded when they realized Mays had turned a certain run into a miracle inning-ending double play." Giant secretary Eddie Brannick, who had seen thousands of games since the time of John McGraw, said it was the finest play he ever saw. Dodger manager Charlie Dressen said Mays would have to do it again before he would believe it. Furillo said flatly that the play was impossible—and that was that. Willie himself, if pressed, will nominate that throw as his greatest.

In the next inning, score still tied 1–1, Mays singled and Westrum homered and the Giants won it. It is conceivable to make a case that The Throw won the pennant for the Giants, inasmuch as the regular season ended in a tie.

Almost two decades later, fans who were there—and Willie himself—still recall The Throw as his finest moment.

STAN MUSIAL

as told to Bob Broeg

Stan Musial's story is one of the glamorous highlights of the game of baseball. A sore-armed pitching prospect in Class D, discouraged and ready to give up, he was persuaded to try his hitting talents and two years later he was in the majors for a career granted few men in any calling. In 1963 Musial celebrated his twenty-fifth year in organized ball. Honored as no other player in history, Musial still looks and acts much as he did when he came to the big leagues from his home town, Donora, Pa. in the late '30s. His records fill an entire page in the record book; he has won Most Valuable Player honors in the National League three times, has led the loop in hitting seven times.

Musial was named general manager of the St. Louis Cardinals in 1967 and in his rookie year at the job saw the club win the National League pennant and the World Series.

THE FLAG atop the right field foul pole at Braves Field was stretched due east. The wind, for once, was blowing out toward the Charles River, which fringes the outfield, instead of coming in like a gale toward home plate. And a St. Louis writer traveling with the Cardinals nudged me on the dugout steps, pointed and grinned. But I just shook my head.

Ordinarily my bats would have jumped for joy in the dugout rack, and I would have looked forward eagerly to taking advantage of the friendly elements, but for two reasons I wasn't happy that chilly afternoon in late September, 1948.

For one thing, we had our backs against the wall because one more victory for the Braves would clinch Boston's first National League pennant since 1914. For another, both my wrists were swollen, sore and throbbing, and batting normally as pleasant a digging into a thick steak, seemed a distasteful and painful chore.

Three days earlier in Brooklyn I had hurt my left wrist playing one of the greatest defensive games of my career. In center field at Ebbets Field, where I've always hit the hardest and most consistently, I raced back to the wall for an "unconscious" gloved catch and charged in for two somersaulting snatches, the second of which saved the bacon in the eighth inning. It was on that play, tumbling over after lunging to pluck the ball off the grass, that I jammed the wrist of my throwing hand.

The left wrist began to hurt at once, but I forgot it temporarily in the good-natured by-play of the clubhouse afterward. Chiding me because I had failed that day for one of the rare times to get one or more blows at Brooklyn, Captain Terry Moore, the old defensive master whose big shoes I was trying to fill in center, punched me in the ribs in the shower and said, "If you only could hit, you might make the team."

The next day we moved over to the Polo Grounds to play the Giants a double-header, and there one of the New York pitchers—names aren't important where accidents are concerned—let a fast ball get away from him, and the ball hit me on the right wrist. Man, that hurts right now.

So into Boston we went for the last stand, and overnight that right wrist began to ache as much as the left. The first day the Braves just about hammered the last nail in our coffin, sweeping a double-header, and I hardly could swing a bat, getting just two hits in both games. I was mighty blue then, as I've mentioned, because I had looked forward to playing on my fifth pennant-winning team—no, you never get tired of winning—and, too, the best season of my career was being hurt by my inability to take a good grip, swing and tee off.

By the time the wind blew toward the right field bleachers that late September afternoon, I had given up my slightest hopes of hitting .400, though I eventually finished with .376, the highest to lead the National League in more than ten years, and I already was assured of finishing first in every offensive department except home runs, a title I lost by one. There was one record, however, that still interested me.

Back in 1922 the one and only Ty Cobb had four outstanding days in each of which he came up with five hits, and that mark had remained unchallenged ever since. Fred Lindstrom and Lefty O'Doul had come closest in the National League with three five-hit days in one season, and I had tied our league's record as early as July 23—and right in Boston, too.

Earlier I had five-hit games in Cincinnati and Brooklyn, and in that July night game at Braves Field I got a chance to tie the N. L. mark and win a ball game at the same time. I had connected safely four times when, one run behind in the ninth inning, we filled the bases with two out and me on deck. As I started up to the plate, Billy Southworth changed pitchers, switching from a right-hander to southpaw Clyde Shoun.

During the delay while Shoun came in to warm up, I started back to the visitors' dugout to change bats and at the steps leading down to the bench, arms folded as usual, Manager Eddie Dyer met me. Unsmiling, Dyer said, "I'm sorry, kid, but I'm afraid I'll have to send up a hitter for you."

I had started back toward the plate and did a doubletake on that one, whirling to find Dyer and the whole bench laughing at the rib. Then I hit Shoun's first pitch right past him into center field for my fifth base hit in a row, scoring two runs and winning the game.

But that was July 23, this was September 22, and in between another five-hit day or night had eluded me. It's tough to get five hits even when you're feeling like a million. You have to be hitting good, but you need some breaks, too, because you can't walk and you can't lose any hits on tough luck. I remember a game earlier that season at Pittsburgh, always my toughest park to hit in. I had "4 for 4" going into the ninth inning when I sent a hot line drive right back at he box, and Bob Chesnes, a good fielding pitcher, reached out and grabbed it.

Now we were through with batting practice, of which I had taken little because the wrists hurt so much. Then I decided to rip off the adhesive tape that seemed so binding it eliminated the little snap I had left. And with Warren Spahn, Boston's great left-hander, due to pitch the Boston "pennant clincher," I made up my mind to try to hit to left field. The pain was too intense when I tried to pull a ball. Besides, I couldn't snap the wrists the way I ought to when going for right field.

The first time up I looped a single to short left field. Spahn, fortunately, was pitching me away, and fortunately, too, he wasn't having one of his good days. In the third inning he put the ball outside again, and high, and I belted a double over the left fielder's head. That was Warren's last inning, incidentally, and when I came up in the fourth the Boston pitcher was Charley (Red) Barrett.

The talkative Barrett, one of baseball's best jockeys, had been giving us the needle from the Boston dugout. As an old former teammate he was digging in the spurs, reminding us what he would do with the big World Series share we'd miss. And now he was out there in a relief role, a "cute" pitcher, as we call his kind—not fast enough to break an egg most of the time, but sneaky enough to slip one past you now and then, and a cagey thrower with plenty of control.

Nibbling at the corner, Red just missed with his first two pitches. Then, behind on the ball-and-strike count, he figured that I would be looking for his "fast" ball or slider. Instead, he served up a change of pace, but it wasn't a good one. The slow one was high, it hung and didn't fool me, and quickly I said "to heck with the wrists" and swung for the right field fence. The wind I previously hadn't been able to use helped now, and the ball sailed into the bleachers for my 38th home run.

By the time I batted in the sixth, the third Boston pitcher was Shoun, and I was paying the piper for the full cut I had taken against Barrett. The wrists seemed on fire, and I poked a pitch on the ground between third base and shortstop, just past Al Dark's outstretched glove. That made it four hits in a row, and because we had a big lead and Boston's flag-wrapping appeared certain to have to wait another day at least, I began thinking about the record seriously.

One more chance, I wanted, and it came against Al Lyons, a wild right-hander Southworth seldom used. Lyons threw and was wild. Ball one. He pitched again. Ball two. My heart

THE BOX SCORE
(September 22, 1948)

St. Louis (N)	A.B.	R.	H.	P.	A.	Boston (N)	A.B.	R.	H.	P.	A.
Schoendienst, 2b.	5	1	1	2	1	Holmes, rf.	3	0	1	1	0
Marion, ss.	5	0	1	2	6	Dark, ss.	4	0	0	2	2
Musial, rf., lf.	5	3	5	4	0	M. McCormick, cf.	4	0	0	4	1
Slaughter, lf.	2	1	1	0	0	Elliott, 3b.	4	0	0	1	1
Northey, rf.	2	0	1	0	0	F. McCormick, 1b.	4	0	0	8	2
Dusak, rf.	0	0	0	1	0	Conatser, cf.	4	1	2	3	0
Jones, 1b.	5	1	2	12	0	Masi, c.	4	0	2	4	0
Moore, cf.	5	0	1	2	0	Sisti, 2b.	4	0	0	2	0
Lang, 3b.	5	1	3	0	3	Spahn, p.	0	0	0	0	1
Rice, c.	4	0	1	4	0	a Sturgeon	1	1	1	0	0
Brazle, p.	4	1	1	0	4	Barrett, p.	0	0	0	0	0
						Hogue, p.	0	0	0	0	0
						b Ryan	1	0	0	0	0
						Shoun, p.	0	0	0	0	1
						Lyons, p.	1	0	0	2	1
Totals	42	8	17	27	14	Totals	34	2	6	27	9

a Tripled for Spahn in 3rd.
b Popped out for Hogue in 5th.

St. Louis (N)	0	1	2	4	0	1	0	0	0—8
Boston (N)	0	0	1	0	0	0	1	0	0—2

Errors—Musial, Jones, Holmes. Runs batted in—Rice, Slaughter, Jones, Marion, Musial 2, Northey, Dark, Masi. Two base hits—Musial, Lang 2, Schoendienst, Northey, Conaster, Masi. Three base hit—Sturgeon. Home run—Musial. Double play—Hogue, Elliott and F. McCormick. Left on base—St. Louis 9, Boston 6. Bases on balls—Brazle 1, Barrett 1, Hogue 1. Strikeouts—Brazle 4, Spahn 1, Barrett 1, Shoun 1. Hits off—Spahn 6 in 3, Barrett 4 in 2-3, Hogue 2 in 1 1-3, Shoun 3 in 2, Lyons 2 in 2. Wild pitch—Shoun. Losing pitcher—Spahn. Umpires—Robb, Pinelli and Gore. Time—1:54. Attendance—10,937.

began to sink as I feared a walk that would deprive me of the last chance I wanted. The players on our bench and in the bullpen were on their feet, pulling for me and needling Lyons to get the ball over, and I made up my mind that while any other time I'd take a pass if it was for the good of the ball club, I'd swing this time at anything, and to blazes with the wrists or where I hit the ball.

The next pitch was close enough, though to this day I couldn't tell you whether it was in the strike zone. I swung, pulling the pitch, and sent a sharp ground ball toward right field. For a fraction of a second, as I dropped the bat and started for first base, I wondered humbly whether the ball would get through, but then I saw it—white against the green grass—bouncing along in the outfield.

Five for five, a fourth time, tying Cobb's old major league record!

Musial's big-league career spans several generations of ball players. He probably would have difficulty remembering the various managers for whom he played, all of whom received one hundred per cent effort from Stan the Man. Men he played with in the '40s are now receiving baseball pensions, others have entered the Hall of Fame, others are no longer on the scene.

Musial has managed to move serenely through the years, getting his hits, smashing his homers, which totaled 463 after the 1962 campaign. He is sixth on the all-time list in this respect, and first among the active players.

An amazing fact of Musial's career as he pushes toward the mid-forties is his enthusiasm for the game. "I like to play as much today as the day I first started," he says. "If I didn't I wouldn't be doing it."

Since Stan the Man has several million dollars cushioning him against any financial bumps or misadventures there is only one course open: you have to believe him.

MEL OTT

as told to John P. Carmichael

*Stumpy Melvin Thomas Ott, born March 1, 1909, in
Gretna, Louisiana, spent all his major league life with
the New York Giants. In 22 active years, Master Mel
cracked 511 homers and drove in 1860 runs, top National League records. Ott also managed the Giants for
six years before joining the club's scouting staff. In 1951
he went to the minors for the first time, when he
assumed the field leadership of the Oakland club of the
Pacific Coast League. He died in 1958.*

CAN A fellow change his mind? You know for quite a few
years I always remembered the day in 1926 that I reported
to the Giants in Sarasota, when I was 16 years old, as my
greatest thrill; when I first saw John McGraw and heard
him say: "Go to the outfield, young man." I wondered afterward how I even had the courage to say a word . . . why
didn't I just nod my head and run quick. Instead I heard
myself: "But I'm a catcher, Mr. McGraw," and he didn't
even seem to be looking at me when he came back:

"That's all right, Bresnahan always thought he was a
pitcher, too!"

Can I change my mind again? Up to the night of August
7, 1940, in the Polo Grounds, whenever anybody asked me
my greatest day it was that afternoon in Washington in
1933 when I hit the home run that gave us the World
Series; when I saw ol' Dolph Luque break a curve off so
sharp to Joe Kuhel for the strike which gave us the cham-

pionship that Gus Mancusco had to dig it out of the dirt. But since August 7, 1940, I know what it means to have an outstanding day to remember. That was Mel Ott night with 53,000 fans in the stands.

All the things that I'd done in baseball for myself just seemed swallowed up in what the fans were doing for me that evening. I'll always be grateful to Mr. Stoneham for picking a regularly scheduled Brooklyn-Giant game for my night, because neither he nor myself wanted to use me to get people out . . . to swell the crowd. The Dodgers and Giants at night would draw anyhow, anytime, so nobody could say we were building up a gate.

I told my wife, before I left for the park, that she'd be lucky if I didn't fall down going after a ball or strike-out with the winning run on third and disgrace her, because I was as nervous as a cat. I've been knocked down and got up again and never thought a thing about it, but I knew there'd be speeches and gifts and I was as tense inside as could be. It's a little embarrassing at that, even though you know the fans mean it and you feel pretty proud. People had been contributing dimes and nickels and more to the committee and my wife knew in advance what I was going to get and she was tickled to death with the gifts. I didn't blame her after I saw 'em. In the cluhouse the boys were calling me the grand old man of the Giants. . . . I was 31 . . . and prophesying that Freddy Fitzsimmons, who was gonna pitch for Brooklyn, would fan me all night long. That's usually the way.

Well, finally we were around the plate and there were flowers all over and then came the gifts. You know what I got? Honestly, it was enough to make a guy choke up. I got a set of flat silver, 208 pieces, a coffee and tea set imported from England, a silver water pitcher, a complete set of golf clubs and bag (they were from the players) a couple of plaques and a gold card of membership in the Baseball Writers Association of America. Carl Hubbell presented the clubs, only it should have been the other way 'round. I ought to have been up there saying those things about him and the rest of the gang.

It was a relief to get the game started. Just as I walked to the plate the first time, a guy with a foghorn voice from upstairs bellowed: "You were a nice guy a little while ago, Ott, but you're a bum beginning now." He must have been a

Dodger rooter and, after all, they were only five games behind the Reds at the time. Ol' Hub was pitching for us and you couldn't ask for a more perfect setup for the customers . . . Hubbell against Fitzsimmons who used to be one of us. For Hub to win meant more to me than anything else, but I wasn't much help to him . . . only one hit in five times up and I made the last out in the ninth after Brooklyn had won, 8–4, but even a homer then wouldn't have helped us.

They got five runs in the seventh and the only thing I did at all was in the fifth when Camilli hit one four country miles. I could see the ball going straight for the Giant bull pen and I just ran automatically and finally jumped at the last minute and it stuck in my glove. It made me feel good because at the time we were leading 4–3 and at least our fans got a chance to yell. Funny about a game like that; chances are most of the folks came out to see two great rivals play, but they'd sort of included me in the celebration.

While we were changing pitchers in the seventh I looked around those stands with fans yelling and laughing and I thought what an ungrateful guy a ballplayer could be who didn't just give everything he had all the time to people who only asked just that and were willing to even make a hero out of him. I never was what you'd call colorful, meaning I just tried to play hard and hit and give my best. You either have a flair of color or you don't and Bill Terry used to kid me lots and say:

"Why don't you do something . . . go get drunk . . . disappear for a few days . . . roll over and catch a ball . . . come into the plate on your hands?"

But that wouldn't have been me and he knew it, too. One time I got a job in a New Orleans clothing store. Didn't have to do a thing but hang around from about 11 A.M. until 3 in the afternoon and I was being overpaid. How could I earn it? Nobody came in to buy suits from the fellow . . . they just wanted to talk baseball. He didn't get any good out of it, so I quit.

Well, to get back to my biggest day, you'd think that I'd gotten everything a fellow could get in one night, but when the game was over and we were going home, there still was more to come. Way back when I first started to play ball, I went with a semipro club in Patterson, Miss. It was owned by a lumberman named Harry Williams, who wanted a camp team and it was Williams who sent me up to McGraw. They were old friends and so I've always had him to thank for my chance. Williams later married Marguerite Clark, the movie actress.

So I got home, with all my presents, and you can imagine how my wife acted over the silver and things and there was a special delivery letter for me. It was from Miss Clark. Williams had died about six years before. The letter said:

"Do you mind if I add a little something to the gifts which all Giant fans are proud and happy to contribute? If Harry were alive, he would want me to do this I know. It would have made him very happy."

It arrived the next day . . . a salad set to match our silver.

JACKIE ROBINSON

as told to Harold Rosenthal

A controversial, exciting figure on and off the playing field, Jackie Robinson became the first Negro to enter baseball's Hall of Fame in 1962. His entire ten years in the majors were spent in the service of the Dodgers, and he also was the first Negro to win Most Valuable Player honors (1949).

Robinson excelled in all phases of baseball: running, hitting and fielding. In college, Robinson was an All-American halfback for the University of California at Los Angeles.

Jackie now works for Governor Nelson Rockefeller's New York State Commission for Human Rights as a full-time aide, holds a position in a Harlem bank and is active in politics.

MY GREATEST thrill in baseball didn't come from any ball I hit, from any base I stole or from any play I made. It came when I heard the national anthem played just before the start of the 1947 World Series, my first World Series.

They lined us Dodgers up along the third base line and put the Yankees along the first base line. Then they played The Star-Spangled Banner and the flag went up out there on the Yankee Stadium flagpole in center field. I don't remember much else about this particular game except that we lost it. But what happened before the game gave me the biggest thrill in my life.

But I guess the game that gave me the most satisfaction,

135

and was about the greatest I played in was that one in Shibe Park on August 10, 1949. It was the night I hit the homer off Jim Konstanty. It was the first time I ever got a hit off him. The homer I got won the ball game.

I remember there was a lot of talk about whether Konstanty should have pitched to me or not. There were two out and one man on and first base was open at the time. The score was tied and Konstanty went ahead and pitched to me instead of walking me like a lot of people thought he should have. I think he did right. You don't walk a man intentionally when he's never gotten a hit off you.

We hadn't been going too good against the Phillies. The night before I had picked up a bad bruise on my left heel during a double steal. We had run on Ken Trinkle, the old Giant relief pitcher, and when Gene Hermanski went down to second base, I took off for home. I beat the throw by plenty, so that I didn't even have to slide. Maybe it would have been better if I had gone down in the dirt because when I ran across the plate instead I took a long, funny kind of a tagging step and came down hard on my heel.

Right away I knew I had done something to it because it hurt like blazes. I didn't get much sleep that night and the next day I could hardly put my foot down on the ground. I stayed in there, though, and that night I got a hit in my second trip to the plate off Ken Heintzelman.

In the game I want to tell you about, we got out in front in the first few innings, thanks to the way Carl Furillo was banging the ball, but around the sixth or seventh they came up and tied it. Then they used a pinch hitter for Heintzelman and when the ninth inning came around it was Konstanty, a fellow who looked good against us all year.

It looked like another good night for Konstanty. Pee Wee Reese and Billy Cox were the first two batters and he got them on infield rollers. Then Furillo banged a single into left field, and went to second on Konstanty's bad pick-off throw, if I remember right. That gave me a shot at him.

I don't remember whether it was eight, nine or ten times I had tried to get a hit off Konstanty during the season and couldn't. But that night it was different. I think it was one ball and one strike and then he let me have my best kind of pitch, one just over the letters on my shirt.

THE BOX SCORE
(*August 10, 1949*)

BROOKLYN	A.B.	R.	H.	P.	A.	PHILADELPHIA · (N)	A.B.	R.	H.	P.	A.
Reese, ss.	5	0	1	3	3	Ashburn, cf.	3	2	2	0	0
Cox, 3b.	4	0	1	1	1	Hamner, ss.	3	1	1	1	3
Furillo, rf.	5	2	3	4	0	Nicholson, rf.	3	1	0	3	0
Robinson, 2b.	3	2	2	2	6	Ennis, lf.	3	0	1	3	1
Hodges, 1b.	4	1	1	6	2	Jones, 3b.	4	0	0	1	5
Edwards, c.	4	1	1	3	0	Goliat, 1b.	3	0	0	8	0
Brown, lf.	3	1	1	1	0	Konstanty, p.	1	0	0	0	0
Hermanski, lf.	1	0	0	1	0	Lopata, c.	4	1	1	5	1
Olmo, cf.	3	0	0	4	0	Miller, 2b.	2	0	0	2	1
Snider, cf.	1	0	1	0	0	Sisler, 1b.	2	0	0	4	0
Branca, p.	3	0	1	1	0	Heintzelman, p.	2	0	1	0	1
Banta, p.	1	0	0	1	0	Blattner, 2b.	2	0	0	0	1
Totals	37	7	12	27	12	Totals	32	5	6	27	13

BROOKLYN	0	0	0	4	1	0	0	0	2—7
PHILADELPHIA (N)	0	0	3	0	0	0	2	0	0—5

Errors—Hamner, Brown, Konstanty. Runs batted in—Ennis 3, Ashburn, Hamner, Edwards 2, Brown 2, Furillo, Robinson 2. Two base hits—Ashburn, Furillo, Lopata, Ennis. Home runs—Brown, Robinson. Stolen base—Robinson. Double plays—Heintzelman, Hamner and Goliat; Reese, Robinson and Hodges. Left on base—Brooklyn 7, Philadelphia 4. Bases on balls—Heintzelman 2, Branca 4. Strikeouts—Heintzelman 2, Branca 3, Konstanty 1. Hits off—Branca 6 in 6 2-3, Banta 0 in 2 1-3, Heintzelman 9 in 7, Konstanty 3 in 2. Hit by pitcher—Heintzelman (Robinson). Winning pitcher—Banta. Losing pitcher—Konstanty. Umpires—Stewart, Conlan and Warneke. Time 2:13. Attendance—16,426.

I swung, and the next thing I knew, the ball was gone, right into the seats, way out in left field. That's a pretty good carry in Shibe Park. I was glad it was a homer instead of any other kind of hit. My foot was aching so badly I could hardly put any weight on it. I don't know what I'd have done if I had to run at top speed or try to slide.

Konstanty then struck out Hodges, the next batter but the two runs in that inning gave us the ball game, because the Phillies couldn't do anything in their half of the ninth. I never got another hit off Konstanty after that but the way things turned out I didn't mind it too much.

Jackie Robinson had a great many thrills coming after those early years. And he provided thrills to the customers with his base running, his ability to inspire the Dodgers to come from behind in the late segments of a game. One season he stole home five times.

Robinson's appearance opened major-league careers to Negroes, and when he hung up his playing equipment after 1956, all clubs in the majors had Negroes on their rosters. Ironically, it was another Negro, Jim Gilliam, who forced Robinson off his second base position and had him finish his career as a third-baseman, outfielder. Robinson made the Hall of Fame the first year he was eligible, with the writers putting ability over all other considerations.

BABE RUTH

as told to John P. Carmichael

*George Herman Ruth left the playground of a Balti-
more orphanage to become the greatest home run hitter
of all time and baseball's most flamboyant figure. He
was born in Baltimore, February 6, 1895. Ruth hit 741
homers in league play, 15 in World Series competition,
and his 1927 total of 60 is still the top mark for a
154-game season. Ruth entered the major leagues as a
pitcher with the Boston Red Sox in 1915, and established a record for the most consecutive scoreless
innings pitched in World Series play with 29⅔ before
turning his unlimited talents to the outfield. He scaled
Olympian heights with the New York Yankees, 1920–
1934, and played his last season in 1935 with the Boston
Braves. The Babe died in New York, August 16, 1948.*

NOBODY BUT a blankety-blank fool would-a done what I
did that day. When I think of what-a idiot I'd a been if
I'd struck out and I could-a, too, just as well as not because
I was mad and I'd made up my mind to swing at the next
pitch if I could reach it with a bat. Boy, when I think of
the good breaks in my life . . . that was one of 'em!

Aw, everybody knows that game; the day I hit the homer
off ol' Charlie Root there in Wrigley Field, the day, October 1, the third game of that 1932 World Series. But right
now I want to settle all arguments: I didn't exactly point to
any spot, like the flagpole. Anyway, I didn't mean to. I just
sorta waved at the whole fence, but that was foolish enough.

All I wanted to do was give that thing a ride . . . outta the park . . . anywhere.

I used to pop off a lot about hittin' homers, but mostly among us Yankees. Combs and Fletcher and Crosetti and all of 'em used to holler at me when I'd pick up a bat in a close game: "Come on, Babe, hit one." 'Member Herb Pennock? He was a great pitcher, believe me. He told me once: "Babe, I get the biggest thrill of my life whenever I see you hit a home run. It's just like watchin' a circus act." So I'd often kid 'em back and say: "O.K., you bums . . . I'll hit one." Sometimes I did; sometimes I didn't . . . but what the heck, it was fun.

One day we were playin' in Chicago against the White Sox and Mark Roth, our secretary, was worryin' about holdin' the train because we were in extra innings. He was fidgetin' around behind the dugout, lookin' at his watch and I saw him when I went up to hit in the 15th. "All right now." Mike Cvengros was pitchin' and I hit one outta the park. We made the train easy. It was fun.

I'd had a lot of trouble in '32 and we weren't any cinches to win that pennant, either, 'cause old Mose Grove was tryin' to keep the Athletics up there for their fourth straight flag and sometime in June I pulled a muscle in my right leg chasin' a fly ball. I was on the bench about three weeks and when I started to play again I had to wear a rubber bandage from my hip to my knee. You know, the old Babe wasn't getting any younger and Foxx was ahead of me in homers. I was 11 behind him early in September and never did catch up. I wouldn't get one good ball a series to swing at. I remember one whole week when I'll bet I was walked four times in every game.

I always had three ambitions: I wanted to play 20 years in the big leagues. I wanted to play in 10 World Series, and I wanted to hit 700 home runs. Well, '32 was one away from my 20th year and that series with the Cubs was No. 10 and I finally wound up with 729 home runs, countin' World Series games, so I can't kick. But then along in September I had to quit the club and go home because my stomach was kickin' up and the docs found out my appendix was inflamed and maybe I'd have to have it out. No, sir, I wouldn't let 'em . . . not till after the season anyway.

The World Series didn't last long, but it was a honey.

That Malone and that Grimes didn't talk like any Sunday school guys, and their trainer . . . yeah, Andy Lotshaw . . . he got smart in the first game at New York, too. That's what started me off. I popped up once in that one, and he was on their bench wavin' a towel at me and hollerin': "If I had you, I'd hitch you to a wagon, you pot-belly." I didn't mind no ball-players yellin' at me, but the trainer cuttin' in . . . that made me sore. As long as they started in on me, we let 'em have it. We went after 'em and maybe we gave 'em more than they could take 'cause they looked beat before they went off the field.

We didn't have to do much the first game at home. Guy Bush walked everybody around the bases. You look it up and I'll betcha 10 bases on balls scored for us. Anyway, we got into Chicago for the third game, that's where those Cubs decided to really get on us. They were in front of their home folks and I guess they thought they better act tough.

We were givin' (the Cubs) hell about how cheap they were to Mark Koenig only votin' him a half-share in the Series and they were callin' me big belly and balloon-head, but I think we had 'em madder by givin' them that ol' lump-in-the-throat sign . . . you know, the thumb and finger at the windpipe. That's like callin' a guy yellow. Then in the very first inning I got a hold of one with two on and parked it in the stands for a three-run lead and that shut 'em up pretty well. But they came back with some runs and we were tied 4 to 4 going into the fifth frame. You know another thing I think of in that game was the play Jurges made on Joe Sewell in that fifth . . . just ahead of me. I was out there waitin' to hit, so I could see it good and he made a helluva pickup, way back on the grass, and "shot" Joe out by a half-step. I didn't know whether they were gonna get on me any more or not when I got to the box, but I saw a lemon rolling out to the plate and I looked over and there was Malone and Grimes with their thumbs in their ears wiggling their fingers at me.

I told Hartnett: "If that bum (Root) throws me in here, I'll hit it over the fence again," and I'll say for Gabby, he didn't answer, but those other guys were standing up in the dugout, cocky because they'd got four runs back and everybody hollerin'. So I just changed my mind. I took two strikes and after each one I held up my finger and said: "That's one" and "that's two." Ask Gabby . . . he could hear me. Then's when I waved to the fence!

No, I didn't point to any spot, but as long as I'd called the first two strikes on myself, I hadda go through with it. It was damned foolishness, sure, but I just felt like doing it and I felt pretty sure Root would put one close enough

THE BOX SCORE
(October 1, 1932)

NEW YORK	A.B.	R.	H.	P.	A.	CHICAGO	A.B.	R.	H.	P.	A.
Combs, cf.	5	1	0	1	0	Herman, 2b.	4	1	0	1	2
Sewell, 3b.	2	1	0	2	2	English, 3b.	4	0	0	0	3
Ruth, lf.	4	2	2	2	0	Cuyler, rf.	4	1	3	1	0
Gehrig, 1b.	5	2	2	13	1	Stephenson, lf.	4	0	1	1	0
Lazzeri, 2b.	4	1	0	3	4	Moore, cf.	3	1	0	3	0
Dickey, c.	4	0	1	2	1	Grimm, 1b.	4	0	1	8	0
Chapman, rf.	4	0	2	0	0	Hartnett, c.	4	1	1	10	1
Crosetti, ss.	4	0	1	4	4	Jurges, ss.	4	1	3	3	3
Pipgras, p.	5	0	0	0	0	Root, p.	2	0	0	0	0
Pennock, p.	0	0	0	0	1	Malone, p.	0	0	0	0	0
						May, p.	0	0	0	0	0
						Tinning, p.	0	0	0	0	0
						Gudat	1	0	0	0	0
						Koenig	0	0	0	0	0
						Hemsley	1	0	0	0	0
Totals	37	7	8	27	13	Totals	35	5	9	27	9

Gudat batted for Malone in 7th.
Koenig batted for Tinning in 9th.
Hemsley batted for Koenig in 9th.

NEW YORK	3	0	1	0	2	0	0	0	1—7
CHICAGO	1	0	2	1	0	0	0	0	1—5

Errors—Lazzeri, Herman, Hartnett, Jurges (2). Runs batted in—Ruth (4), Gehrig (2), Cuyler (2), Grimm, Chapman, Hartnett. Two-base hits—Chapman, Cuyler, Jurges, Grimm. Home runs—Ruth (2), Gehrig (2), Cuyler, Hartnett. Stolen base—Jurges. Double plays—Sewell to Lazzeri to Gehrig, Herman to Jurges to Grimm. Struck out—By Root, 4; by Malone, 4; by May, 1; by Tinning, 1; by Pipgras, 1; by Pennock, 1. Bases on balls—Off Root, 3; off Malone, 4; off Pipgras, 3. Hit by pitched ball—By May, 1. Hits—Off Root, 6 in 4 1-3 innings; off Malone, 1 in 2 2-3 innings; off May 1 in 1 2-3 innings; off Tinning, 0 in 2-3 innings; off Pipgras, 9 in 8 innings; off Pennock, 0 in 1 inning. Winning pitcher—Pipgras. Losing pitcher—Root. Umpires—Van Graflan (A.L.), Magerkurth (N.L.), Dineen (A.L.), and Klem (N.L.). Time—2:11. Attendance—49,986.

for me to cut at, because I was showin' him up. What the hell, he hadda take a chance as well as I did or walk me!

Gosh, that was a great feelin' . . . gettin' a hold of that ball and I knew it was going someplace . . . yes sir, you can feel it in your hands when you've laid wood on one. How that mob howled. Me? I just laughed . . . laughed to myself going around the bases and thinking: "You lucky bum . . . lucky, lucky" and I looked at poor Charlie (Root) watchin' me and then I saw Art Fletcher (Yankee coach) at third wavin' his cap and behind him I could see the Cubs and I just stopped on third and laughed out loud and slapped my knees and yelled: "Squeeze-the-Eagle-Club" so they'd know I was referrin' to Koenig and for special to Malone I called him "meat-head" and asked when he was gonna pitch.

Yeah, it was silly. I was a blankety-blank fool. But I got away with it and after Gehrig homered, behind me, their backs were broken. That was a day to talk about.

GEORGE SISLER

as told to Lyall Smith

George Sisler, born March 23, 1893, in Manchester, Ohio, was one of baseball's top stars. His .420 average in 1922 is still the highest seasonal batting figure in the American League. A powerful and timely batter, skillful fielder and cunning base stealer, Sisler was truly outstanding in all departments. Pitcher, first baseman, outfielder and left-handed throwing second baseman, George achieved his finest seasons with the St. Louis Browns from 1915 through 1927. Associated with Branch Rickey, his discoverer, since closing out his active playing career in 1930. Sisler is now a talent man for the Pittsburgh Pirates.

EVERY AMERICAN kid has a baseball idol. Mine was Walter Johnson, the "Big Train." Come to think about it, Walter still is my idea of the real baseball player. He was graceful. He had rhythm and when he heaved that ball in to the plate he threw with his whole body just so easy-like that you'd think the ball was flowing off his arm and hand.

I was just a husky kid in Akron (Ohio) High School back around 1910–11 when Johnson began making a name for himself with the Senators and I was so crazy about the man that I'd read every line and keep every picture of him I could get my hands on.

Naturally, admiring Johnson as I did, I decided to be a pitcher and even though I wound up as a first baseman my biggest day in baseball was a hot muggy afternoon in St.

Louis when I pitched against him and beat him. Never knew that, did you? Most fans don't. But it's right. Me, a kid just out of the University of Michigan beat the great Walter Johnson. It was on August 29, 1915, my first year as a baseball player, the first time I ever was in a game against the man who I thought was the greatest pitcher in the world.

I guess I was a pretty fair pitcher myself at Central High in Akron. I had a strong left arm and I could throw them in there all day long and never have an ache or pain. Anyway, I got a lot of publicity in my last year in high school and when I was still a student I signed up to play with Akron.

I didn't know at the time I signed that contract I was stepping into a rumpus that went on and on until it finally involved the National Baseball Commission, the owners of two big league clubs and Judge Landis.

I was only 17 years old when I wrote my name on the slip of paper that made me the property of Akron, a club in the Ohio-Pennsylvania League and a farm club of Columbus in the Association. After I signed it I got scared and didn't even tell my dad or anybody 'cause I knew my folks wanted me to go on to college and I figured they'd be sore if they knew I wanted to be a ball player.

In a way, that's what saved me, I guess. For by not telling my dad he never had a chance to okay my signature and in that way the contract didn't hold. The way it worked out Akron sold me to Columbus and Columbus sold me to Pittsburgh and all the time I was still in high school and hadn't even reported to the team I signed with! Wasn't even legally signed the way it turned out.

They wanted me to join the club when I graduated from high school but I was all set to go to Michigan so I said "no" and went up to Ann Arbor. Well, to make a long story short the story came out in the open then and when the whole thing was over I had been made a free agent by the old National Commission and signed up with Branch Rickey who at that time was manager of the St. Louis Browns.

I pitched three years of varsity ball up at Michigan and when I graduated on June 10, 1915, Rickey wired me to join the Browns in Chicago. Now, all this time I was up at school I still had my sights set on Walter Johnson. When he pitched his 56 consecutive scoreless innings in 1912 I was as proud as though I'd done it myself. After all, I felt as though I had adopted him. He was my hero. He won 36 games and lost only seven in 1913 and he came back the next season to win 28 more and lose 18. He was really getting the headlines in those days and I was keeping all of them in my scrapbook.

Well, then I left Michigan in 1915 and came down to Chicago where I officially became a professional ballplayer. I hit town one morning and that same day we were getting beat pretty bad so Rickey called me over to the dugout.

"George," he said, "I know you just got in town and that you don't know any of the players and you're probably tired and nervous. But I want to see what you have in that left arm of yours. Let's see what you can do in these last three innings."

I gulped hard a couple of times, muttered something that sounded like "thanks" and went out and pitched those last three innings. Did pretty good, too. I gave up one hit but the Sox didn't get any runs so I figured that I was all right.

Next day, though, I was out warming up and meeting more of the Browns when Rickey came over to me. He was carrying a first baseman's glove. "Here," he said. "Put this on and get over there on first base."

Nothing much happened between the time I joined the club in June until long about the last part of August. Rickey would pitch me one day, stick me in the outfield the next and then put me over on first the next three or four. I was hitting pretty good and by the time we got back to St. Louis the sports writers were saying some nice things about me.

They were saying it chiefly because of my hitting. I'd only won two-three games up to then. I still remember the first one. I beat Cleveland and struck out nine men. Some clothing store gave me a pair of white flannels for winning and I was right proud of them.

As I was saying, we got back to St. Louis late in August. Early one week I picked up a paper and saw that a St. Louis writer, Billy Murphy, had written a story about Washington coming to town the following Sunday and that Walter Johnson was going to pitch.

I was still a Johnson fan and Murphy knew it, for when I got halfway through the story I found out that he had me pitching against Johnson on the big day, Sunday, August 29.

That was the first I knew about it and I figured it was the first Manager Rickey knew about it, for here it was only Tuesday and Murphy had the pitchers all lined up for the following Sunday.

Wel, he knew what he was talking about, because after the Saturday game Rickey stuck his head in the locker room and told me I was going to pitch against Johnson the next day. I went back to my hotel that night but I couldn't sleep. At 4:00 A.M. I was tossing and rolling around and finally got up and just sat there, waiting for daylight and the big game.

I managed to stick it out, got some breakfast in me and was out at Sportsman's Park before the gates opened. It was one of those typical August days in St. Louis and when game time finally rolled around it was so hot that the sweat ran down your face even when you were standing in the shadow of the stands.

All the time I was warming up I'd steal a look over at Johnson in the Washington bull pen. When he'd stretch 'way out and throw in a fast ball I'd try to do the same thing. Even when I went over to the dugout just before the game started I was still watching him as he signed autographs and laughed with the photographers and writers.

Well, the game finally started and I tried to be calm. First man to face me was Moeller, Washington's left fielder. I didn't waste any time and stuck three fast ones in there to strike him out. Eddie Foster was up next and he singled to right field. Charley Milan singled to right center and I was really scared. I could see Mr. Rickey leaning out of the dugout watching me real close so I kept them high to Shanks and got him to fly out to Walker in center field. He hit it back pretty far though and Foster, a fast man, started out for third base. Walker made a perfect peg into the infield but Johnny Lavan, our shortstop, fumbled the relay and Foster kept right on going to score. That was all they got in that inning, but I wasn't feeling too sure when I came in to the bench. I figured we weren't going to get many runs off Johnson and I knew I couldn't be giving up many runs myself.

Then Johnson went out to face us and I really got a thrill out of watching him pitch. He struck out the first two Brownies and made Del Pratt fly to short center. Then I had to go out again and I got by all right. In the second

THE BOX SCORE
(August 29, 1915)

WASHINGTON	R.	H.	P.	A.	ST. LOUIS	R.	H.	P.	A.
Moeller, lf.	0	0	2	0	Shotton, lf.	0	0	0	0
Foster, 2b.	1	2	3	3	Auston, 3b.	0	2	2	1
C. Milan, cf.	0	1	0	0	Pratt, 2b.	0	0	4	3
Shanks, 3b.-rf.	0	1	0	1	Walker, cf.	1	1	4	0
Gandil, 1b.	0	1	6	3	Jacobson, rf.	1	1	1	0
Johnson, p.	0	1	1	1	Howard, 1b.	0	1	9	1
Williams, c.	0	1	1	1	Lavan, ss.	0	0	3	5
McBride, ss.	0	0	5	1	Severeid, c.	0	1	4	1
Acosta, rf.	0	0	1	0	Sisler, p.	0	1	0	1
Morgan, 3b.	0	0	0	0					
H. Milan, rf.	0	0	0	0					
Totals	1	7	19	11	Totals	2	7	27	12

WASHINGTON	1	0	0	0	0	0	0	0	0—1
ST. LOUIS	0	2	0	0	0	0	0	0	x—2

Errors—Williams, Lavan (2). Sacrifice hits—Williams, Pratt, Lavan, Johnson, Moeller. Double plays—Lavan to Howard (2); Severeid to Austin. Bases on balls—Off Sisler, 2. Hit by pitched ball—Acosta by Sisler; Sisler by Johnson. Struck out—By Johnson, 6; Sisler, 3.

inning, Walker led off with a single to center field and Baby Doll Jacobson dumped a bunt in front of the plate. Otto Williams, Washington catcher, scooped it up and threw it 10 feet over the first baseman's head. Walker already was around second and he came in and scored while the Baby Doll reached third.

I think I actually felt sorry for Johnson. I knew just how he felt because after all, the same thing had happened to me in the first inning. Del Howard was next up for us and he singled Jacobson home to give us two runs and give me a 2–1 lead.

Well, that was all the scoring for the day, although I gave up five more hits over the route. Johnson got one in the first of the fifth, a blooper over second. I was up in the last of the same inning and I'll be darned if I didn't get the same kind. So he and I were even up anyway. We each hit one man, too.

There wasn't much more to the game. Only one man reached third on me after the first inning and only two got that far on Johnson.

When I got the last man out in the first of the ninth

and went off the field I looked down at the Washington bench hoping to get another look at Johnson. But he already had ducked down to the locker room.

I don't know what I expected to do if I had seen him. For a minute I thought maybe I'd go over and shake his hand and tell him that I was sorry I beat him but I guess that was just the silly idea of a young kid who had just come face to face with his idol and beaten him.

WARREN SPAHN

as told to Bob Ajemian

Greatest left-handed winner in the history of the National League, Warren Spahn was born in Buffalo, New York, April 23, 1921. He won 363 big league games, 350 of them for the Braves, first in Boston and later in Milwaukee. He holds the major league record for most seasons as a 20-or-more winner, and holds the National League record for home runs by a pitcher. At the tail end of his career, he was pitcher-coach for the New York Mets and later the San Francisco Giants. In 1967 he became manager of Tulsa in the Pacific Coast League.

BROOKLYN NEEDED one game to clinch the pennant. I needed that same game to reach 20 wins. It was a day late in September, Ebbets Field was jam-packed as I walked out to the mound, and if you want to know why this was my greatest game, listen to me.

I had 16 wins the day we left Boston for our last Western trip of the 1947 season. Sixteen wins, ten losses, and the string was running out.

I've been on a pennant winner since then, the 1948 team; I've pitched in a World Series, but even now in looking back, winning that 20th game in 1947 was the greatest challenge and thrill I've received out of baseball.

It was early in September when the Braves began their final trip of the year. On the train I figured out how many starts I'd probably have left. If Billy (Southworth) kept working me in my regular turn, I counted on five more.

Johnny Sain was chasing his 20th win just like I was.

Of course, he had won 20 the year before. He was ahead of me now, about one or two games. I think he had 18 when we left Boston. He finished up with 21 for the season, I remember that.

The difference between winning 19 games and winning 20 for a pitcher is bigger than anyone out of baseball realizes. It's the same for hitters. Someone who hits .300 looks back on the guy who batted .295 and says "tough luck buddy."

Twenty games is the magic figure for pitchers; .300 is the magic figure for batters. It pays off in salary and reputation. And those are the two things that keep a ballplayer in business.

Well, the first town we hit was Cincinnati. I was as ready as I'll ever be. We won, 3 to 0. I was strong, had plenty of stuff.

The last out was a fly to Tommy Holmes in right field. He came running in afterwards, handed me the ball and said:

"That's 17, Spahnny. You're off now."

My next chance came in St. Louis. Again I was pretty hot. We beat the Cards, 5 to 0, another shutout. I grabbed the game ball and tucked it away. Things felt pretty good that night.

The 19th victory, four days later, was against Chicago in Wrigley Field. We won, 1 to 0, my third shutout in a row. I was finally in that slot, one before 20. The pressure was really on now, and I could feel it.

I wanted to ask Billy how many more starts I'd get, but I decided against it. The Braves had recalled some kid pitchers from the minors, and I figured they would be looking them over. But Billy came through for me.

He told me I was going to pitch against the Dodgers on September 21. I told myself:

"It will be your last chance. Don't count on any more. This is the one you'll have to win. They've got too many kids they want to test."

My wife, Lorene, flew down from Boston to be with me. She had been writing to me all the time while we were on the road, and I knew she was going through the same feeling I was.

The night before the game, we sat in our room together in the Hotel Commodore. I said to her:

"Brooklyn needs only one win to clinch the pennant.

Every Dodger fan in New York will probably want to be there tomorrow to see them do it. Branca's going to pitch, did you see the paper? He's won 21 already."

"Let's not talk about the game," she said to me. Lorene was as nervous as I was.

But the payoff came the next afternoon just before the game. If anything could have upset the applecart, this would have been it.

Lorene and I allowed plenty of time to get to the ball park. We took the subway from the Commodore, hoping, of course to get off in Brooklyn. Instead we were let off in the Battery. The subway only went as far as the bridge that day and stopped.

We hurried out to a cab and headed for the Brooklyn Bridge. The going was slow, the lights seemed to be against us all the way. Lorene didn't say a word, but I could see she was getting jumpy. All I could think about was getting there on time.

After a long ride, we finally got near the ball park. What a mob. The place was sold out completely. Everybody had turned out to see Brooklyn clinch the pennant.

They had the whole place roped off to prevent people with no tickets from getting anywhere near the ball field.

And I had no ticket. We don't need them at the players' entrance. But the players' entrance was 100 yards away, past a crowd of people, a rope, and some tough-looking policemen.

My wife and I barged through, got to the rope, and were pushed back by a cop.

"But I'm a ballplayer," I started to argue. He gave me a quick answer and a half-shove back.

"So am I," he said. "An' we're gonna do all our playin' right out here. Now get on with you and don't be disturbin' me."

"But I'm with the Boston club and I have to pitch today," I said to him. "I'm late already."

"Listen buddy, I'm from Brooklyn and so are you. Now get movin'."

He was starting to get mad, I could see that. If I had said anything else, there's no telling what he might have done.

This is where my wife stepped in. She went right under the rope and after him. If it hadn't been for her, Brooklyn might have clinched the pennant that day, and I might never have—well let me tell you.

The next thing I heard was:

"Pardin' me madam, but how was I to know you were Mrs. Spahn." We were ushered over to the entrance.

But I had even more trouble when I finally walked onto the mound.

It wasn't the capacity crowd that bothered me, even though they were yelling like the mischief. It was a strong wind coming out of New York harbor and blowing from the first base side of the plate out toward left field—a sort of crosswind.

It made my curve ball break just too wide of the plate. It took me only two batters to find out. I tried using my change-up, and that kept coming in too low. The wind was too strong.

I'm a control pitcher. That's my strength, and if my control is off, I might as well throw underhand. I had walked only nine batters in the last 77 innings I had pitched before this game.

In the first four innings that afternoon, five Dodgers got bases on balls.

The first inning was rough. I loaded the bases, with walks to Stanky and Reese and an error on Bruce Edwards' grounder. Two men were out and Dixie Walker was the hitter.

I got him to ground to Connie Ryan at second.

In the second inning, with men on first and third, two men out, I struck out Jackie Robinson.

In the third inning with Reese on third base, two out, I got Walker on a change-up. He popped a short fly to 'Bama Rowell in left field.

I felt good. And I kept telling myself:

"This has got to be the one. You won't get another chance after today."

It seemed to be paying off.

In our half of the fourth, Torgy (Earl Torgeson) doubled and Dick Culler scored him with a single.

In their fourth, Don Lund, a rookie outfielder, was the first batter. The wind was still bothering me. I walked him. Then Spider Jorgenson smashed a ball between first and second. It looked like a hit.

Torgy raced over and made a dive for the ball. He turned

a somersault in the air, no kidding a complete somersault. And he came up sitting on the ground.

He threw the ball over to me from his sitting position. I raced across the first base bag. I could feel Jorgenson's foot hit the bag after mine.

But Scotty Robb—some name for an ump, huh?—called him safe. It upset me a lot because I felt we had made the play. Especially after Torgy's stop.

Branca then tried to sacrifice. He popped a bunt foul a few feet outside the third base line. Bob Elliott, you know how big he is, sprinted over from third the same as I did from the mound.

I reached out for the ball, felt it in my glove, then collided with Bob.

They told me in the dugout afterwards we both started spinning like tops. Elliott did a full spin and fell right on his back. He crashed down on his head. I spun a couple of times, but kept my balance, and also luckily kept the ball.

The first thing I saw when my eyes stopped blinking was Elliott. He was lying flat on the ground. The next thing I saw was Lund. He was trying to sneak from second to third after the catch. And the third thing I saw was Phil Masi, our catcher, streaking down to cover third.

I was off balance, but threw to Masi anyway. It was about knee-high and to the far side of the bag. Phil tumbled to his knees, reached out beyond the bag for the ball and grabbed it. He put it on Lund for the double play.

Everything was happening.

We got two more in the fifth when Masi doubled two runners in.

I had a three-run lead to work with. The pressure was off. Someone told me after the game I had made 86 pitches in the first four innings. I made only 18 in the next two.

In the seventh, Stanky and Reese singled with two out. I walked Carl Furillo to load the bases and you should have heard the crowd yell when Edwards stepped into the box.

He was late on a fast ball and popped to Ryan at second.

The walk to Furillo was the last one I gave. I was used to the wind a little more by now and fooled around with some pitches.

My wife was sitting right in back of the Braves' dugout. I hadn't dared to look at her before the seventh. When Edwards popped up, I glanced at her before walking into the dugout. She had a big smile; I think she realized how confident I felt by then.

We won, 4 to 0. The Dodgers only got six hits, Reese got three of them. It was my fourth shutout in a row, my 20th win of the season.

Every guy on that team shook my hand after the game. Even the fans who had come looking for a Dodger pennant that afternoon gave me a big hand as I walked off the field. It was the biggest game of my life.

*   *   *

It's funny how certain things which happen in baseball will always stick with a guy, especially a pitcher who must learn to accept both victories and defeats as the inevitable in approximately 35 to 40 games. Yet there are always one or two contests which can never slip from a fellow's memory. And so it is that for as long as I'm capable of remembering clearly and vividly, never will I forget a lazy, sunshiny spring day, again at Ebbets Field, in 1951, when I pitched —and lost—one of my greatest games.

The season was only five days old and I had already dropped my first start, a toughie to the Giants, when I took the mound to face the Dodgers that Monday afternoon. April 23rd was the date, a forever memorable one since it also was my twenty-ninth birthday, but sixteen innings and three hours and fifty-three minutes later I realized that Brooklyn wasn't going to allow me to celebrate.

Joe Hatten was my pitching opponent at the outset, and he gave up the first run—and the only one we were to score in sixteen innings—in the third inning. My catcher, Ray Mueller, slashed a line drive into left field, good for two bases, and Buddy Kerr's single moved him to third base. Then I topped a roller down the first-base line, and Ray just did beat Gil Hodges' toss to the plate for our lone tally.

The first four innings were easy enough for me, and I still had a run lead until that big Hodges came up in the fifth and blasted one deep into those friendly left-field seats. From then on the game belonged to the pitchers.

As the zeros plopped out on the scoreboard inning after inning I honestly felt I could go on until we were forced to catch our train for the next town. The Dodgers weren't giving me too much trouble, but our boys weren't exactly wearing the ball out either, and the Brooklyn pitchers—

there were three of them that day—were just as stubborn about staying out in the sun.

For years left-handers were regarded as erratic individuals, to be babied, perhaps, and looked upon with a certain indulgence at least. Certainly they were not expected to perform with the consistency of right-handers.

From the fifth to the fifteenth innings I turned in ten scoreless frames, but never did get the eleventh.

The sixteenth stanza started harmlessly enough. I retired Pee Wee Reese on a foul fly, but then Billy Cox rifled an honest single to left and moved to second when pitcher King sacrificed. So there were two out, the winning run on second and pinch-hitter Eddie Kiksis at the plate, still not too ominous a situation. And then Miksis banged a grounder at Gene Mauch, who had replaced Sid Gordon at third base. Our outfielders started to throw away their gloves and come in for their licks in the seventeenth inning. But there were to be no more innings played that day! The usually sure-fingered Mauch bobbled the bounder and now the Dodgers had their winning run on third and a man on first.

Before the next Brooklyn batter, Carl Furillo, a right-handed swinger, got to the plate, Billy Southworth dashed out of the dugout with those brisk steps of his and was at my side suggesting that I pass Furillo in order to pitch to the lefty-hitting Duke Snider. I knew Billy's counsel was sound and in keeping with the pitching percentages, but I was a trifle leery of walking Furillo to load the bases, and then maybe being forced to come in with a "fat" pitch to Snider if I got behind on the count. So I pitched to Furillo, but carefully, and then with a two-two count on him Carl blasted a real beauty to the top of the scoreboard for the game-winning blow.

Warren Spahn changed all that. His big-league career which actually started in 1947, has had very few peaks or bottoming outs. He has fanned more than 100 batters for sixteen straight seasons, a record. He pitched in 246 or more innings for sixteen straight years, another unmatched mark.

He never has started less than 32 times a season, has led the National League in complete games eight time. All in all, Spahn adds up to the highest-paid pitcher in history, a World Series performer, and a man with a bright future at the age of 42.

THE BOX SCORE
(September 21, 1947)

BOSTON (N)	A.B.	R.	H.	P.	A.		BROOKLYN	A.B.	R.	H.	P.	A.
Holmes, rf.	5	1	3	5	0		Stanky, 2b.	4	0	1	1	2
Hopp, cf.	3	0	0	2	0		Robinson, 1b.	5	0	0	6	1
Rowell, lf.	4	1	1	3	0		Reese, ss.	5	0	3	0	2
Elliott, 3b.	5	0	0	0	11		Furillo, cf.	2	0	0	2	0
Torgeson, 1b.	3	2	1	4	0		Edwards, c.	3	0	0	9	0
Masi, c.	4	0	1	6	0		Bragan, c.	0	0	0	2	0
Ryan, 2b.	4	0	0	2	2		Walker, rf.	4	0	0	1	0
Culler, ss.	4	0	2	4	2		Lund, lf.	2	0	0	6	0
Spahn, p.	2	0	0	1	1		Jorgensen, 3b.	4	0	2	0	2
							Branca, p.	2	0	0	0	0
							a Lavagetto	1	0	0	0	0
							Hatten, p.	0	0	0	0	1
							b Miksis	1	0	0	0	0
							Behrman, p.	0	0	0	0	0
Totals	34	4	8	27	16		Totals	33	0	6	27	8

a Flied out for Branca in 7th.
b Popped out for Hatten in 8th.

```
BOSTON (N)     0 0 0 1 2 0 1 0 0—4
BROOKLYN       0 0 0 0 0 0 0 0 0—0
```

Error—Rowell. Runs batted in—Culler, Masi 2. Two base hits—Reese, Torgeson, Masi. Sacrifice—Hopp. Double play—Spahn and Masi. Left on base—Boston 10, Brooklyn 12. Bases on balls—Spahn 6, Branca 5, Hatten 1. Strikeouts—Spahn 5, Branca 7, Hatten 1, Behrman 1. Hits off—Branca 8 in 7, Hatten 0 in 1, Behrman 0 in 1. Wild pitch—Spahn. Winning pitcher—Spahn. Losing pitcher—Branca. Umpires—Pinelli, Robb, Gore. Time—2:35. Attendance—34,123.

TRIS SPEAKER

as told to Francis J. Powers

Tristram Speaker moves in exclusive company. He's the third man in baseball's all-time, all-star outfield. Born August 4, 1888, in Hubbard City, Texas, the "Grey Eagle" was baseball's finest defensive outfielder, and only Cobb before him ever established a higher league lifetime batting average. The silver-thatched Speaker glittered for 20 years, starting with the Red Sox before moving on to Cleveland, where he managed for eight years. Tris keeps active as a tutor for the Indians during the spring training period and as a Texas oil man the year-round.

I'LL ALWAYS think of the 1912 season as one of the greatest in major league history. That's natural for it was in 1912 that I first played with a pennant winner and world's championship team, and there are no greater thrills for a young player. Our Boston Red Sox, managed by Jake Stahl, a former University of Illinois star, won the American League pennant while the New York Giants were the winners on the National League side.

There were a couple of great teams. The Red Sox won 105 games that season for a league record that stood until the Yankees won 110 in 1926. And the Giants came home with 103 victories and no other National League winner since touched that total until the Cardinals won 106 in 1942. Joe Wood won 34 games for us, almost one-third of our total and 10 of them were shutouts.

Many a time I have heard "Smoke" say in our clubhouse meetings, "Get me two runs today and we'll win this one." Woody won 16 in a row and beat Walter Johnson after the Big Train had won a similar string and no one has beaten those marks although they have been tied. We had Duffy Lewis and Harry Hooper in the outfield and there never were any better, Larry Gardner at third, Heinie Wagner at short and Buck O'Brien and Hugh Bedient on the pitching staff, just to mention some of our stars.

While Wood (and Johnson) made pitching history in the American League that summer Rube Marquard was writing an unequaled chapter in the National. The gangling, wiry-necked left-hander won 19 straight and no one has come along to wipe out that performance. Those Giants were a hard hitting, fast running team with the likes of Josh Devore, Red Murray, Buck Herzog, Chief Meyers and Fred Merkle and had great pitchers in Christy Mathewson, Marquard, Jeff Tesreau and Red Ames.

In the opening game of the World Series Woody beat Tesreau, 4 to 3. I guess maybe John McGraw figured "Smoke" would beat any of his pitchers so he held Marquard and Mathewson back; although Tesreau was a great pitcher. The second game went 11 innings to a six-all tie with Matty pitching for the Giants and Bedient, Ray Collins and Charlie Hall, who died a few weeks ago, working for Boston. In the third game the Giants made it all even with Marquard getting a 2–1 decision over O'Brien. Then Wood and Bedient beat Tesreau and Mathewson in terrific 3–1 and 2–1 duels and we were ahead three games to one and it looked as if the series was about finished.

But the Giants weren't through by any means. In the sixth game, Marquard beat O'Brien and Collins and in the seventh, the Giants took a toe hold and pounded Wood out of the box and kept on hammering O'Brien and Collins to win 11–4. So the Series went into its eighth game on October 16 and that's where I had my biggest day.

McGraw called on Christy Mathewson with the chips down and that was natural for Matty still was in his prime; his fadeaway was tough to hit and he knew every angle of the pitching business. Since Wood already had worked three games, and had been beaten the day before Stahl couldn't send him back, so he started Bedient.

The game quickly took the form of a magnificent pitcher's

battle and I don't think that Matty ever was much better than that autumn afternoon. He turned us back with machinelike precision for six innings and by that time the one run the Giants had scored in the third began to look awful big. I got a double into right field in the first inning but through six innings that was about our only scoring chance. The Giants got their run when Devore walked, advanced on two outs and scored when "Red" Murray hit a long double. That the Giants weren't another run to the good in the fifth was due to one of the greatest catches I ever saw. Larry Doyle hit a teriffic drive to right that appeared headed for a home run but Harry Hooper cut it off with a running, leaping catch that was easily the outstanding play of the Series.

Boston tied the score in the seventh due to confusion among the Giants. Stahl hit a Texas leaguer toward left and it fell safe when Murray, Fred Snodgrass and Art Fletcher couldn't agree on who was to make the catch. Wagner walked and then Stahl sent Olaf Hendrickson up to bat for Bedient. Now Hendrickson was one of the greatest pinch hitters ever in the game; like Moose McCormick of the Giants. He was one of those rare fellows who could go up cold and hit any sort of pitching. Matty worked hard on Hendrickson but the Swede belted a long double that scored Stahl. Then Joe Wood came in to pitch for us.

The score still was one-one going into the 10th and the Giants tried their best to put the game away in their half. Murray doubled again and he was the tough man for us all through the Series and raced home on Lerkle's single. So there we were behind again with the last chance coming up.

Once more the breaks and big breaks went our way. Clyde Engle batted for Woody and reached second when Snodgrass muffed his fly in center field. And I was the next batter.

It looked as if I was out when I cut one of Matty's fadeaways and lifted a high foul between the plate and first base. The ball was drifting toward first and would have been an easy catch for Merkle. I was going to yell for Meyers to make the catch for I didn't think he could, but before I could open my mouth I heard Matty calling: "Meyers, Meyers."

Meyers chased the ball but it was going away from him and finally Merkle charged in but he was too late and couldn't hold the ball. Fred was blamed for not making the catch and the term "bonehead" was thrown at him again,

THE BOX SCORE
(October 16, 1912)

NEW YORK

	A.B.	R.	H.	P.	A.
Devore, rf.	3	1	1	3	1
Doyle, 2b.	5	0	0	1	5
Snodgrass, cf.	4	0	1	4	1
Murray, lf.	5	1	2	3	0
Merkle, 1b.	5	0	1	10	0
Herzog, 3b.	5	0	2	2	1
Meyers, c.	3	0	0	4	1
Fletcher, ss.	3	0	1	2	3
McCormick	1	0	0	0	0
Mathewson, p.	4	0	1	0	3
Shafer, ss.	0	0	0	0	0
	—	—	—	—	—
Totals	38	2	9	*29	15

BOSTON

	A.B.	R.	H.	P.	A.
Hooper, rf.	5	0	0	3	0
Yerkes, 2b.	4	1	1	0	3
Speaker, cf.	4	0	2	2	0
Lewis, lf.	4	0	0	1	0
Gardner, 3b.	3	0	1	1	4
Stahl, 1b.	4	1	2	15	0
Wagner, ss.	3	0	1	3	5
Cady, c.	4	0	0	5	3
Bedient, p.	2	0	0	0	1
Hendrickson	1	0	1	0	0
Wood, p.	0	0	0	0	2
Engle	1	1	0	0	0
	—	—	—	—	—
Totals	35	3	8	30	18

* Two out when winning run scored.

McCormick batted for Fletcher in 9th.

Shafer went to shortstop in 10th.

Hendrickson batted for Bedient in 7th.

Engle batted for Wood in 10th.

NEW YORK	0	0	1	0	0	0	0	0	0	1—2	
BOSTON	0	0	0	0	0	0	1	0	0	2—3	

Errors—Doyle, Snodgrass, Speaker, Gardner (2), Stahl, Wagner. Two-base hits—Murray (2), Herzog, Gardner, Stahl, Hendrickson. Sacrifice hit—Meyers. Sacrifice fly—Gardner. Stolen base—Devore. Struck out—By Mathewson, 4; by Bedient, 2; by Wood, 2. Bases on balls—Off Mathewson, 5; off Bedient, 3; off Wood, 1. Hits—Off Bedient, 6 in 7 innings; off Wood, 3 in 3 innings. Winning pitcher—Wood. Umpires—O'Loughlin (A.L.), Rigler (N.L.), Klem (N.L.) and Evans (A.L.). Time—2:39. Attendance—17,034.

recalling his failure to touch second base in 1908. I never thought Merkle deserved any blame at all. It was Matty who made the blunder in calling for Meyers to try for the catch.

That gave me a reprieve and I didn't miss the second chance. I got a good hold of a pitch for a single to right that scored Engle and the game was tied again. Then Matty walked Lewis, purposely, for Duffy always was a money hitter, filling the bases. With Gardner at bat the Giant infield played in close on the chance of cutting Yerkes off at the plate. But Gardner was another who did his best when the chips were on the table and crashed a long fly that sent Yerkes home with the deciding run.

I was in other World Series, but outside of the game between Cleveland and Brooklyn in 1920, when Bill Wambsganss made his unassisted triple play, I can't recall any when there was more drama and when there were more unusual incidents. It was a great thrill for me to manage the Cleveland Indians to the 1920 world's championship, with my mother looking on; but from strictly a playing angle, that single off Matty was my biggest moment.

CASEY STENGEL

as told to John P. Carmichael

*"Oldest man in uniform" is the proud boast of the sep-
tuagenarian Casey Stengel, a World Series manager
whose five straight titles with the Yankees, 1949–53,
should stand long after he is gone. An outfielder who
never forgot anything he learned, Stengel suffered
through a long managerial drought before coming to
his career with the Yankees, a career which made him
a national figure on and off the field. Fired by the
Yankees after the 1960 season because he was "too
old," Casey came back in 1962, after writing his life
story, to manage the New York Mets in their fledgling
years. When he broke his hip in July of 1965, he was
forced to retire. He still scouts for the Mets on the West
Coast where he lives and is president of a Glendale,
California, bank.*

TWO BALLPLAYERS lolled on a bench one day in Kankakee,
Ill., in 1910, watching the antics of a teammate in the outfield.
The object of their gaze would haul down a fly ball, throw
it into the infield, then sail his glove ahead of him on the
grass, take a run and slide into the mitt. "He won't be with
us long," observed one onlooker. "You mean he's going up?"
asked the other. "No," replied the first, "there's an institu-
tion here to take care of guys like that . . . !"

I WAS only practicing three things at once (said Stengel) like
running, throwing and sliding. And I fooled them, because

two years later, in September, I got off a train in New York, a brand new suitcase in one hand and $95 in my pocket. The next day was my greatest in baseball. I was reporting to Brooklyn. Is that 30 years ago? I must be getting old.

The bag was Kid Eberfield's idea. He was back from the majors and playing with us at Montgomery, Ala., in the Southern League when Manager Johnny Dobbs gave me the offer to join the Dodgers. The Kid and Mrs. Eberfield came over to say good-by and good luck while I was packing. I had one of those cardboard valises . . . they'd last about 1,000 miles if you got good weather, but if you ever got caught in the rain with one, you'd suddenly find yourself walking along with just a handle in your hand.

Well, they told me I couldn't go to the big leagues with a thing like that and made me lay out $18 for a good one. I'd gone two and a half years to dental school and I was trying to save up enough tuition dough for another year. It cost about $150 plus more for instruments and I was short enough without buying a bag. "You won't come back," said Eberfield. "Never mind the money. Forget about being a dentist."

So I got to New York. It was in the evening and no use going to the park then, so I asked a cab-driver for a place to stay and he drove me to the Longacre Hotel at 47th St. I checked in and went down and sat in the lobby. I was afraid to go out, it was so dark, but finally I walked down to 46th St. and then hustled back, for fear I'd get lost. About 20 minutes later I went as far as 45th and back. I kept adding another block each trip and had been clear to 42d St. and returned by midnight when I decided to turn in. Next morning I started for the park. Brooklyn played then at the old Washington St. grounds at 5th Av. and 3rd and with the help of an elevated and a streetcar I made it. The gateman found out what I wanted and waved toward the clubhouse. "Go on down there," he said . . . and, as I walked away, he called after me: "You better be good."

I'll never forget walking into the locker room. There was a crap game going on in one corner. The only fellow who paid any attention to me was Zack Wheat. He introduced me around. Nobody shook hands. Some grunted. A few said hello. I walked over to the game and decided maybe I ought to get in good with the boys by participating in their sport, so I fished out $20 and asked if I could shoot. Somebody said:

"Sure," and handed me the dice. I rolled 'em out. A hand reached for my 20 and a voice said: "Craps, busher," and I never even got the bones back. I was about to reach for more money when I felt a tap on my shoulder and there was Manager Bill Dahlen.

"Are you a crapshooter or a ballplayer, kid?" he asked. I told him I was a player and he said: "Well, get into a suit and on that field while you still have carfare." I hustled, believe me, and I've never touched dice since. I got to the bench and just sat there. I knew better than to pick up a bat and go to the plate. Eberfield told me what happened to rookies who tried that. Finally Dahlen came over and said: "Let's see you chase a few" and I ran like hell for the outfield. Behind the fence was a big building with fire escapes all down one side and guys in shirt sleeves were parked on the steps, passing around pails of beer and getting set for the game.

I never expected to play, but just as the umpire came out Dahlen told me to "get in center." Hub Northern, the regular center fielder, had been sick, and I guess they decided they might as well get me over with quick. My first time at bat we had a man on first and Dahlen gave me the bunt sign. The pitch wasn't good and I let it go by. Claude Hendrix, the league's leading pitcher was working for Pittsburgh and George Gibson catching. Hendrix threw another and I singled to right-center. When I got to the bench after the inning Dahlen stopped me. "Didn't you see the bunt sign?" he asked. I told him yes, but that down South we had the privilege of switching on the next pitch if we wanted to. "I don't want you to carry too much responsibility, kid," he said, "so I'll run the team and all you'll have to worry about is fielding and hitting." My ears were red when I got to center field.

Up on the fire escape the boys were having drinks on my hit and I could hear them speaking real favorably of me. I heard somebody holler and it was Wheat telling me to move back. Hans Wagner was at the plate. He larruped one and I went way back and grabbed it. In the dugout Wheat said: "Better play deeper for him." I thought of the catch I'd made and said to myself: "I can grab anything he can hit." Two innings later he came up again and Wheat waved me back, but I wouldn't go and wham! old Hans peeled one off. The ball went by me like a bee bee shot and he was roosting on third when I caught up with it.

I got three more hits right in a row. The first time Hendrix had fed me a fast ball, figuring why waste his best pitch, a spitter on a busher. He was pretty mad by the time I combed two blows off his spitter and another off his hook. Once when I was on first Dahlen gave me the steal sign and away I went. I beat Gibson's throw and Wagner just stood there, looking down at me. Never said a word. I stole two bases and when I came up the fifth time we'd knocked Hendrix out and a left-hander was pitching for the Bucs. Manager Fred Clark hollered at me: "All-right, phenom, let's see you cross over." I was feeling cocky enough to do it. . . . I stepped across the plate and stood hittting right-handed and damned if I didn't get a base on balls.

The Dodgers were playing the Cubs two days later when Stengel came to bat with nobody on. Cub Catcher Jimmy Archer looked up at him and said: "So you're the new Brooklyn star, huh? A base-stealer, too, huh? Well, I hope you get on and go down." Stengel got on and, with two out, Dahlen gave him the green light. "I was 20 feet from the bag when I saw Johnny Evers with the ball," said Casey. "I tried to slide around him, but no use. He really crowned me. As I lay there, he pulled up one pant leg. 'Oh, tryin' to spike me,' he growled, although I hadn't even touched him. 'I'll stick this ball down your throat if you ever try it again, busher!'"

Stengel's greatest day was over. His education had begun!

JOHNNY VANDER MEER

as told to Gabriel Paul

John Samuel Vander Meer, born November 2, 1914, in Paterson, New Jersey, accomplished a feat unlikely to be repeated in big league baseball—he pitched two successive no-hit, no-run games for Cincinnati in 1938. Never more than a journeyman pitcher because of poor control and arm ailments, Vandy's achievement will stand as the game's most dramatic feat. Vander Meer was traded to the Cubs in 1950 after serving 11 years with the Reds. He then managed for a decade in the minors.

After his retirement from the game, he became a brewery representative in Tampa, Florida.

IT WOULD seem natural for me to name the second successive no-hitter I pitched in 1938 as my biggest day in baseball, and I'll have to explain why it isn't.

Those games were as much a surprise to me as to the baseball world. I wasn't keyed up to their meaning then. Before the no-hitter against Boston on June 11 that year I was just a rookie that nobody but Bill McKechnie knew, and after the June 15 repeat of the performance against Brooklyn I was still just a novelty, a kid who had done a freakish thing.

To understand my feelings at the time you've got to understand that I came up to the Reds that year after an unsuccessful season at Syracuse in the International League. I had won only five and lost eleven for the Chiefs. Nobody thought I was good but Bill McKechnie, manager of the Reds, who told me, when I arrived at spring training in Florida, that he was counting on me to be a regular. He said he believed I could make it.

He gave me hope, and then on the way north that spring in an exhibition series with the Boston Red Sox Lefty Grove gave me some tips on what I was doing wrong. I'll never be able to thank Lefty for his friendliness and smartness in putting his finger on my errors. McKechnie kept giving me great advice, too, all spring.

I'll never forget the day that spring we were at Lynchburg, Va. I was pitching batting practice and after a little while McKechnie, on the bench, began to yell: "He's got it! He's got it! That boy is going to make it!"

That helped more than I can say, and I got off to a pretty good start in the season, pitching a shutout against the Giants at the Polo Grounds on May 20. I had my confidence. I felt I could do it. Then, all at once, came those consecutive no-hitters.

But they came too fast. I was more confused than thrilled. All the publicity, the attention, the interviews, the photographs, were too much for me. They swept me off my feet too far to let me have time to think about the games themselves. There were too many people around me.

As I look back at it now those days are the haziest period of my life—sort of like a dream.

I might have been dreaming then, but I awoke the next season, 1939, when I won five and lost nine. I was sick that spring and never did seem to regain my stride. My confidence went, too. I wasn't much better in the spring of 1940. Bill McKechnie and Warren Giles talked to me about going to Indianapolis of the American Association to regain my confidence. I thought it was a swell idea. I knew that was what I needed. At the same time it made me realize just how quickly a fellow can fall from the pedestal.

My going to Indianapolis was the best thing that ever happened to me. I got off on the right foot there, won six and lost four, had an earned-run average of 2.40 and struck out 109 in 105 innings. That satisfied Giles and McKechnie, for they brought me back for the last stages of the 1940 pennant race.

The Reds were in first place. They were on their way to the pennant, but they hadn't clinched it. I was given an opportunity to start a game and won it. Then we went to Philadelphia September 17, needing only two victories to clinch the pennant. We won on the 17th, then McKechnie gave me another chance to work, on September 18—the day that is my biggest.

I was up against Hugh Mulcahy, one of the smartest and most determined of pitchers and awfully tough when he was in form. We saw right off that he was in form when the game started. Joe Marty, whom the Phils had got from the Cubs, was on a rampage that day, too, getting three hits. And Mulcahy was leveling off with his bat, as well as with his arm. We could get hits, but we couldn't get runs. Mulcahy would turn us back.

The Phils got me for two runs in the second inning, and it was the fifth before we got one run. I began to wonder if I was going to let the team down on the one game it needed to clinch the flag. It was life-and-death in my mind. I had to hang on to my "comeback." I had to win.

We finally tied it in the seventh 2–2, but in the 10th we got one to give us what we thought was the game, but the Phils in their half got one off me to even it up again. It was true I had blanked them the seven innings between the second and the 10th, and the team was all the time telling me how good I was going, but there it was, we'd been ahead and I'd let the Phils tie us.

Was I really a comeback or not? Could I clinch the flag or couldn't I?

I gave everything I had straight through the 11th and 12th innings and blanked them. But we didn't score either and the scoreboard still showed 3–3.

I was up in the 13th at bat and I figured now was the time. All of Mulcahy's pitches were good, but I kept swinging and somehow all at once whistled one into left center, and ran faster than I ever had before, I suppose. I got to second. They sacrificed me to third. Then Mike McCormick hit an infield ball and I was held at third, too risky to chance a run in. Mike beat it out.

Ival Goodman was up. Twice he cracked the ball and I tore for home, only to be called back because the drive went foul. Then he got one fair, a short fly to the outfield and I tagged up and when McKechnie on the coasting line said, "Run, Johnny, run!" to give me the exact moment the ball settled into the fielder's glove, I sure ran. I took off in the hardest slide I ever made and looked up through the dust. The umpire was motioning "safe."

We were ahead.

McKechnie, cool always, looked at me and figured how much running I' ddone that inning, and told me to sit it out, he'd send in Joe Beggs to pitch the last half. Joe got them 1-2-3 and the flag was ours.

HANS WAGNER

as told to Chet Smith

John Peter Wagner, the "Peerless Dutchman," was the first "great" in the National League. Born February 24, 1874, in Carnegie, Pennsylvania, Wagner was a huge, barrel-chested man with long arms and ham-like hands who was flushed out of a Pennsylvania coal mine to achieve an outstanding career as a superlative all-round player. Beginning with Louisville, Honus moved over to Pittsburgh where he played every position but catcher. During 21 years Wagner batted better than .300 in 17 seasons. Hans coached for the Pirates before illness forced him to retire. He died in 1955.

WHEN A fellow has played 2,785 games over a span of 21 years it's not the easiest thing in the world to pick out a single contest and say it was his best or that it gave him his biggest thrill. But I was never sharper than in the last game of the World Series our Pirates played with the Detroit Tigers of 1909, and I never walked off any field feeling happier.

It was the afternoon of October 16 and not only a big day for me but for all the sport fans, for on that same afternoon Big Jack Johnson, heavyweight prize-fight champion, knocked out Stanley Ketchel in the 12th round of their battle in San Francisco to retain his crown.

I regard that final game with the Bengals as tops because it meant the end of a grand fight against a bunch of real fighters. I'm still willing to testify that the club of Hughie Jennings and Ty Cobb, of "Wahoo Sam" Crawford and Donie Bush, of Davy Jones and George Moriarity, was a holy terror. And it tickles my vanity to think the Pirates outbattled and defeated them.

Cobb stole two bases in the series, but I was lucky and got six. Cobb made six hits, I made eight.

Ask Ty what happened the day he stood on first and yelled at me, "Hey, Kraut Head, I'm comin' down on the next pitch." I told him to come ahead, and by golly, he did. But George Gibson, our catcher, laid the ball perfect, right in my glove and I stuck it on Ty as he came in. I guess I wasn't too easy about it, 'cause it took three stitches to sew up his lip. That was the kind of a series it was from start to finsh. Fred Clarke, our manager, told us we'd better sharpen our spikes since the Tigers would be sure to, and we took him at his word. We were sorta rough, too, I guess.

Cobb surprised the Pirates by playing an unusually clean series, but some of the others weren't so careful.

The trouble started in the first game. Both sides had their jockeys warmed up. The Tigers let us have it and we gave it back to 'em with interest. There was a jawing match on nearly every pitch, and it was a good thing we had two of the greatest umpires who ever worked—Bill Klem and "Silk" O'Loughlin. They were young fellows then, but they knew their business and kept us in line. At least there weren't any riots.

In that first game, Fred Clarke hit a home run off Big George Mullin, who was Detroit's best pitcher that year. I followed Clarke at the plate, and I could see that Mullin was boiling, and anxious to get back at us. I always stood pretty far away from the plate, but this time took every inch I could, figuring Mullin would throw at me. I wasn't wrong. He laid his fast ball right in my ribs. Of course, you can't say a thing like that is deliberate, but our boys reckoned it was, and from that minute the rough-housing was on.

We came into the final game tied up at three apiece. It was played in Detroit, and the night before, the Tiger rooters hired two or three bands to play in front of our hotel and keep us awake, But Clarke fooled 'em by taking us all out to a tavern along the lake shore.

We knew our pitcher was going to be Babe Adams, the kid who had won two of our three victories. Babe was hardly old enough to shave, but Clarke had a hunch on him all along. I'll never forget the look on Adams' face when I told

THE BOX SCORE
(October 16, 1909)

PITTSBURGH	R.	H.	P.	A.	DETROIT	R.	H.	P.	A.
Byrne, 3b.	0	0	0	0	D. Jones, lf.	0	1	3	0
Hyatt, cf.	1	0	0	0	Bush, ss.	0	0	3	5
Leach, cf.-3b.	2	2	4	2	Cobb, rf.	0	0	1	0
Clarke, lf.	2	0	5	0	Moriarity, 3b.	0	1	1	0
Wagner, ss.	1	1	3	3	O'Leary, 3b.	0	0	1	1
Miller, 2b.	0	3	3	0	Delehanty, 2b.	0	2	2	3
Abstein, 1b.	1	1	10	0	Crawford, cf.	0	0	4	0
Wilson, rf.	1	0	0	0	T. Jones, 1b.	0	1	9	0
Gibson, c.	0	2	2	1	Schmidt, c.	0	1	3	1
Adams, p.	0	0	0	0	Donovan, p.	0	0	0	1
					Mullin, p.	0	0	0	2
Totals	8	9	27	6	Totals	0	6	27	13

PITTSBURGH	0 2 0 2 0 3 0 1 0—8
DETROIT	0 0 0 0 0 0 0 0 0—0

Error—D. Jones. Hits—Off Donovan, 2 in 3 innings. Three-base hit —Wagner. Two-base hits—Moriarity, Abstein, Leach, Gibson, Schmidt, Miller, Delehanty. Sacrifice hits—Leach. Stolen Bases—Clarke (2), Abstein, Miller. Hit by pitched ball—Byrne, Bush. Struck out—By Adams 1, Mullin 1. Base on balls—Off Adams 1, Donovan 6, Mullin 4. Double play—Bush to Schmidt to Bush. Umpires—O'Loughlin and Klem.

him Clarke wanted him to pitch the opener. He asked me if I wasn't fooling and I told him I wasn't and he hadn't better fool, either, when he got on the mound. What a job he did for us.

I guess I don't have to tell you what the feeling was that last day. "Wild Bill" Donovan, who started for the Tigers, lived up to his name and we got two runs off him in the second. Mullin came in to pitch in the fourth and couldn't find the plate, either. There were two walks and two singles, giving us two more. In the sixth I got my only hit, but it was a three-bagger that drove in Clarke and Tommy Leach, and I kept coming and crossed the plate when Davey Jones made a bad throw from the outfield. We certainly didn't need the run we picked up in the seventh, but it made us eight, and with Adams pitching perfect ball that was the score 8 to 0. But it's far from being the whole story.

On my hit Jones kicked the ball into the overflow crowd, trying to hold it to a double under the ground rules, but O'Loughlin saw him and wouldn't allow it. Another time there was a close play at first and the Tiger runner hit Bill Abstein, our first baseman, in the stomach with his fist. Abstein folded up and Ham Hyatt had to take his place. Another Tiger slid into second and cut Jack Miller on the head and leg. Bobby Byrne, our third baseman, banged into Moriarity so hard that Bobby had to leave the field with a broken ankle, and George, who concealed his injury until the next inning, went to the doctor to have 11 stitches put in his knee. Talk about "bean balls"—they were flying around everybody's head all afternoon.

TED WILLIAMS

as told to Gerry Moore

Third among the all-time homer stars with a mark of 521, Ted Williams brought his distinguished career to an end after the 1960 campaign. He hung up a lifetime mark of .344, batting in a park which scarcely favored his left-handed stance. He was the last major leaguer to bat .400 (406 in 1941).

Williams served with distinction in both World War II and the Korean War as a Marine flier. He was a controversial figure on and off the field and was always a dynamic lure at the box office.

He still retains his connection with the game as a talent scout for the Boston Red Sox, the only team he played for during his career. He also serves as special batting instructor for the Red Sox in spring training, and is given much of the credit for the development of Carl Yastrzemski, the American League's Most Valuable Player in 1967.

I GUESS I've had more than my share of thrills from baseball, but the greatest game in my own book still stands as the one played on Friday the 13th of September in 1946 at League Park in Cleveland.

That was the day I hit my first inside-the-park homer.

That unusual sock for the circuit in the very first inning provided the run that Tex Hughson preserved for a 1–0 victory and the first pennant in 28 years for our Red Sox.

It took some soul-searching on my part to place that incident above the many other great days I've enjoyed during my eight active years in the best game of them all.

Who could forget his first grand slammer? That happened to me on August 19, 1939 in Washington when I clipped Pete Appleton with the bases loaded. The best part of that was it helped us win an 8–6 decision from the Nats.

Then there was the All-Star Game in Detroit in 1941 when I bashed a homer against the top deck in Briggs Stadium with two out and two aboard in the ninth inning off Claude Passeau to give our American Leaguers a 7–5 win for the annual inter-league classic.

For a kid of twenty-two in those days, it was like a dream to be carried off the field on the shoulders of Joe DiMaggio, who had just crossed the plate ahead of me, and Bobby Feller, who was already in civilians after having finished his early three-inning pitching stint. My boyhood idols like Jimmy Foxx and Joe Cronin were mussing up my hair and tearing off my cap all during my free ride to the clubhouse that day.

All those things almost made me forget the record homer I had hit over the whole right field stands in the same Briggs Stadium two years earlier.

Along came the final day of that same 1941 season and we were playing in Philadelphia. After batting above .400 for most of the campaign, I had been whiffed three times on Saturday at Shibe Park by that old knuckle-baller, Roger Wolff, and had fallen just below the .400 mark.

I needed plenty of hits during Sunday's double-header to be sure to finish above that magic figure. I want to take the opportunity right now to thank Mr. Mack for instructing his pitchers on that occasion to pitch to me unless baseball strategy demanded otherwise.

I wound up with "six for eight" during that big twin bill and a .406 figure for the season to become the first major leaguer to join the Four Hundred Club since Bill Terry belted .401 for the Giants back in 1930.

Next, my mind flashed back to the All-Star Game in 1946 at our own Fenway Park when we American Leaguers mauled our old rivals by a 12–0 count. Nobody could ask for a better day than I experienced before most of my home folks when I singled first time up, homered into the center field seats off Kirby Higbe next, lined a single into right, then another off Phil Cavarretta's shins and wound up the day by smacking Rip Sewell's famous "blooper ball" into the right field seats for another fourmaster.

Four hits, including two homers, in four official times-at-bat, four runs and five RBI's certainly represented a full afternoon.

However, only five days later was started the chain of circumstances that finally led me to choose Friday the 13th of September later the same big year as the red letter date on my personal baseball calendar.

In the first game of a double-header on Sunday, July 14th, at the same Fenway Park against the Indians, I connected for three homers in a single game for the first time in my career and batted across eight runs, which still stands as a RBI record for myself.

The third of my homers, which were my 24th, 25th and 26th of that season, provided the winning run for us of an 11–10 slugfest that was otherwise memorable because Lou Boudreau belted four doubles as well as a homer himself.

When I came up for the second time in the second game, which we also won, 6 to 4, Lou introduced the famous shift with which other teams have been trying to plague me ever since.

I managed to get a two-bagger in two official trips while facing the Boudreau shift for the first time, but I really caught up with it on that sweetest of Friday the 13ths in September.

Red Embree was the pitcher that famous day in League Park and I'll have to let eye-witnesses tell you how the Indians were placed the first time I came to bat. Three infielders were to the right of second base. Third Baseman Don Ross was almost on top of the middle bag. Center Fielder Felix Mackiewicz was on the right field side of center. Left Fielder Pat Seerey was almost behind third base, about 20 feet back on the grass and some 15 feet from the foul line.

I lost no time exploring the yawning left-center pasture. I lined Embree's first fat one in that direction and took off around the bases. People later told me that I was almost to third when Mackiewicz retrieved the ball from a gutter in front of the center field bleachers, more than 400 feet from the plate.

I wasn't looking because my heart was in my legs that day. I was thinking about all the years that Tom Yawkey and Joe

Cronin had been trying to give Boston a pennant. There were plenty of us players who were getting tired of finishing second, too.

I finally slid across the plate even though I guess I really didn't need to. I also later learned that Lou Boudreau's relay bounced away from the dish down the third base line and Catcher Jim Hegan had to step down and reach for the ball as I slid across.

After that big game when everybody was celebrating, a writer walked up to me and said: "I guess that's the easiest home run you ever hit, Ted."

"Like fun," I said, "it was the hardest."

My friend asked me why.

"Because I had to run for it," was my answer.

Run or not, it still stands as the greatest game I ever played in my own mind and probably will remain that way until maybe I can do something big to help the Red Sox win a World Series.

THE BOX SCORE
(September 13, 1946)

BOSTON (A)	A.B.	R.	H.	P.	A.	CLEVELAND	A.B.	R.	H.	P.	A.
DiMaggio, cf.	3	0	0	1	0	Mackiewicz, cf.	3	0	0	4	0
Pesky, ss.	3	0	1	2	5	Ross, 3b.	4	0	0	1	2
Williams, lf.	3	1	1	1	0	Seerey, lf.	3	0	1	1	0
Doerr, 2b.	4	0	0	2	4	Edwards, rf.	4	0	0	3	0
York, 1b.	3	0	0	11	1	Fleming, 1b.	4	0	0	8	3
McBride, rf.	4	0	0	6	0	Boudreau, ss.	3	0	0	0	2
H. Wagner, c.	4	0	0	4	0	Mack, 2b.	3	0	1	3	1
Gutteridge, 3b.	2	0	0	0	0	Hegan, c.	3	0	0	6	0
Hughson, p.	3	0	0	0	3	Embree, p.	2	0	1	1	3
Totals	29	1	2	27	13	Totals	29	0	3	27	11

BOSTON (A)	1	0	0	0	0	0	0	0	0—1
CLEVELAND	0	0	0	0	0	0	0	0	0—0

Error—Embree. Run batted in—Williams. Two base hit—Mack. Home run—Williams. Sacrifices—Gutteridge, Mackiewicz. Left on base —Boston 6. Cleveland 5. Bases on balls—Embree 4, Hughson 2. Strike-outs—Hughson 4, Embree 3. Umpires—Grieve, Paparella and Hubbard. Time—1:28. Attendance—3,295.

CARL MICHAEL YASTRZEMSKI

as told by Jack Orr

Carl Michael Yastrzemski was born August 22, 1939, son of a Polish potato farmer in Southampton, Long Island, New York. He played a lot of sandlot ball around that area, drawing attention of a good many scouts. Though he entered Notre Dame, he never played there, being lured to the major leagues by a $100,000 bonus offered by the Boston Red Sox. He was considered to be Ted Williams' successor as slugger extraordinary when he joined the Sox in 1961, but he never achieved much fame in his first six years in the big league. Managers complained that he didn't try very hard, that he was listless, that it didn't seem to bother him that the Red Sox were a perennial second-division team. Then in 1967, under rookie manager Dick Williams, Yastrzemski put all his talents together and was responsible more than any other player for the astonishing Boston pennant victory that year. "He has been the perfect player for me all year," his manager said.

NEVER IN the sixty-seven-year history of the American League had there been the kind of mixed-up race that 1967 produced. With only forty-eight hours remaining before the end of the season that had started six months earlier, the standings looked like this:

	Won	Lost	%	G.B.	To Play
Minnesota	91	69	.569	–	2
Boston	90	70	.563	1	2
Detroit	89	69	.563	1	4
Chicago	89	71	.563	2	2

Detroit was to play two doubleheaders, Saturday and Sunday, with the California Angels. Chicago had two single games with the Washington Senators. And Minnesota was in Boston to play a Saturday game and a Sunday game with the Red Sox. If the Twins did no worse than split their two games at Fenway Park, they were virtually assured of the pennant.

There were a good many surprises that Saturday afternoon. Eddie Stanky's White Sox lost their fourth straight game to Washington. Though they started their superior 16-game-winner, southpaw Gary Peters, they were shut out by the Senators' Frank Bertaina, who was winning only his seventh game of the year. The scoreless Chicago attack marked the 27th inning in a row in which the White Sox failed to get a run.

In Detroit the Tigers had their troubles, too. Despite Mickey Lolich's fine 3–0 three-hit shutout in the first game of the doubleheader, California exploded for six runs in the eight inning of the second game to triumph, 8–6. That defeat made it impossible for the Tigers to do better than tie somebody and force a playoff.

Up in Boston, however, destiny was being fashioned that had the nation's baseball fandom in a state of excitement. The Cinderella Red Sox, underdog favorites of most fans because Boston had risen from a gloomy ninth-place finish the year before, were putting on a magnificent show for the 32,909 customers. Jim Kaat, a splendid lefthander who won 16 games for the Twins, started against the Sox' Jose Santiago.

Minnesota scored first as the game got under way. Zoilo Versalles singled, Harmon Killebrew walked and Tony Oliva singled home the run. Kaat injured his elbow in the third inning and was replaced by Jim Perry, and the Red Sox caught up with him two innings later on hits by Reggie Smith, Dalton Jones, Jerry Adair and—in a clutch situation with two out—a sizzling single by Yastrzemski. Sox 2, Twins 1. Then Minnesota scored to tie in the sixth, but George Scott gave the Red Sox another run with his homer.

Now it was the tense seventh inning and the Boston rooters pleaded for a fatter lead. Young Mike Andrews hit a grounder to short and beat the throw by an eyelash for an infield hit. Versalles booted Adair's sharply hit grounder—and that brought up hero Yastrzemski. He took a curve inside, looked at a fast ball strike and then smashed the next delivery into the distant right field bleachers—a blow that sewed things up for Boston (though Killebrew hit a two-run homer in the ninth off reliever Gary Bell). The homers were No. 44 for both Yaz and Killebrew and they tied for the league leadership. And to put icing on Yastrzemski's cake, No. 44 was more home runs than idol Ted Williams ever hit in a single season.

Now it was Sunday morning, final day of the season, and though the White Sox, by virtue of their defeat in Washington, were mathematically out of it, each of the other three clubs had a chance, thus:

	Won	Lost	%	G.B.	To Play
Minnesota	91	70	.565	–	1
Boston	91	70	.565	–	1
Detroit	90	70	.562	½	2

The Tigers by winning both ends of their doubleheader could tie the winner of the Red Sox-Twins game. That would have entailed a three-game playoff.

In Boston, they shoehorned 35,770 fans into the tiny, antiquated park. The Red Sox' task was formidable. They had to face the brilliant Dean Chance, a 20-game winner and the second best strikeout artist in the league. Boston's starter was Jim Lonborg, the six-foot-six ace of the staff, who had pitched twice within the previous six days.

The Red Sox fell behind early as the jammed stands groaned. The Twins scored in the first inning on a wild throw by George Scott, and they added another in the third on an error by (of all people) Yaz. Boston was having little luck with the deliveries of Dean Chance and they trailed, 2–0, as they came to bat in the sixth.

Lonborg himself started things off with a safe bunt which Cesar Tovar couldn't handle. Adair and Jones followed with sharp singles and the Red Sox had the bases loaded and the hitter was Yastrzemski, who had had two hits—a double and a single—already. Yaz wasted no time as the fans held their collective breath. He slashed a scorching single up the middle, good for two runs. A play at the plate failed for the

THE BOX SCORES

(September 30, 1957)

MINNESOTA	A.B.	R.	H.	RBI.	BOSTON	A.B.	R.	H.	RBI.
Versalles, ss.	5	1	1	0	Andrews, 2b.	3	1	2	0
Tovar, 3b.	5	1	1	0	Adair, 3b.	4	1	1	1
Killeb'w, 1b.	4	1	2	2	Yastrz'ski, lf.	4	1	3	4
Oliva, rf.	5	0	1	1	Harrelson, rf.	3	0	0	0
Allison, lf.	2	1	1	0	Howard, c.	1	0	0	0
Carew, 2b.	4	0	0	0	Scott, 1b.	4	1	2	1
Uhl'nder, cf.	4	0	2	0	Petrocelli, ss.	3	0	0	0
Zim'rman, c.	2	0	0	0	Smith, cf.	4	1	1	0
Reese, ph.	1	0	1	1	Gibson, c.	1	0	0	0
Nixon, c.	1	0	0	0	Jones, ph.	1	1	1	0
Kaat, p.	1	0	0	0	Tartabull, rf.	2	0	0	0
Perry, p.	1	0	0	0	Santiago, p.	3	0	0	0
Kostro, ph.	0	0	0	0	Bell, p.	1	0	0	0
Kline, p.	0	0	0	0					
Merritt, p.	0	0	0	0					
Rollins, ph.	1	0	0	0					
Totals	36	4	9	4	Totals	34	6	10	6

```
MINNESOTA    1 0 0 0 0 1 0 0 2—4
BOSTON       0 0 0 0 2 1 3 0 x—6
```

MINNESOTA

	IP.	H.	R.	ER.	BB.	SO.
Kaat	2⅓	3	0	0	1	4
Perry	2⅔	4	2	2	0	4
Kline (L. 7-1)	1⅓	2	3	3	0	1
Merritt	1⅔	1	1	1	1	0

BOSTON

	IP.	H.	R.	ER.	BB.	SO.
Santiago (W. 12-4)	7	7	2	2	4	7
Bell	2	2	2	2	0	0

E—Versalles. DP—Minnesota 1. LOB—Minnesota 9, Boston 6. 2B—Killebrew, Smith, Tovar. 3B—Uhlaender. HR—Scott (19), Yastrzemski (44), Killebrew (44). U—Honochick, Chylak, Springstead and Drummond. T—3:03. A—32,909.

(October 1, 1967)

MINNESOTA	A.B.	R.	H.	RBI.	BOSTON	A.B.	R.	H.	RBI.
Versalles, ss.	3	0	0	0	Adair, 2b.	4	1	2	0
Reese, lf.	1	0	1	0	Andrews, 2b.	0	0	0	0
Tovar, 3b.	3	1	0	0	Jones, 3b	4	1	2	0
Kil'brew, 1b.	2	2	2	0	Yastr'ski, lf.	4	1	4	2
Oliva, rf.	3	0	2	0	Har'lson, rf.	3	0	0	1
Allison, lf.	4	0	1	1	Tartabull, rf.	1	1	0	0
Hern'dez, ss.	0	0	0	0	Scott, 1b.	4	0	0	0
Uhl'nder, ss.	4	0	1	0	Pet'celli, ss.	3	0	1	0
Carew, 2b.	4	0	0	0	Smith, cf.	4	0	0	1
Zim'rman, c.	2	0	0	0	Gibson, c.	2	0	0	0
Nixon, c.	1	0	0	0	Siebern, ph.	1	0	0	0
Rollins, ph.	1	0	0	0	Howard, c.	1	0	1	0
Chance, p.	2	0	0	0	Lonborg, p.	4	1	2	0
Worth'ton, p.	0	0	0	0					
Kostro, ph.	1	0	0	0					
Roland, p.	0	0	0	0					
Grant, p.	0	0	0	0					
Totals	31	3	7	1	Totals	35	5	12	4

```
MINNESOTA   1 0 1 0 0 0 0 0 1 0—3
BOSTON      0 0 0 0 0 0 5 0 0 x—5
```

MINNESOTA

	IP.	H.	R.	ER.	BB.	SO.
Chance (L. 20-14)	5*	8	5	5	0	2
Worthington	1	0	0	0	1	1
Roland	0†	3	0	0	0	0
Grant	2	1	0	0	0	1

BOSTON

	IP.	H.	R.	ER.	BB.	SO.
Lonborg (W. 22-9)	9	7	3	1	4	5

*Pitched to five batters in sixth.
†Pitched to three batters in seventh.

E—Scott, Yastrzemski, Killebrew. DP—Minnesota 3, Boston 2. LOB—Minnesota 5, Boston 7. 2B—Oliva, Yastrzemski. WP—Worthington 2. U—Honochick, Chylak, Springstead and Drummond. T—2:25. A—35,770.

Twins and Jones scored the third run, the go-ahead run, and Allan Worthington relieved for Minnesota, threw two wild pitches, allowing Yastrzemski to score. Another came in on Killebrew's error at first. The Red Sox were in first place and a hair's breadth from winning the pennant.

For in Detroit, the Tigers had won the first game and were trailing only 4–3 in the second. But Bill Rigney's Angels exploded in mid-innings to take an 8–3 advantage and the Tigers late bid of two runs in the seventh only narrowed the margin to 8–5, and the Red Sox, for the first time in 21 years and only the second time in half a century, were the winners of the American League pennant.

It would be difficult to say that they could have won without the services of their handsome left fielder. He led the American League in hitting with a .326 average; he drove in 121 runs, more than anybody in baseball; he tied for the home run leadership of both leagues; he got more basehits and scored more runs than anyone else in his league, and his slugging percentage of .622 dwarfed all other baseball players in 1967. In the field he was a superb defensive player, making circus catches, cutting off potential extra base hits, slamming vigorously into outfield walls. His arm was a thing to behold and though runners seldom took chances with it, he still was able to achieve more assists than all but two outfielders in his league. In the final game he threw out the potential tying run.

He was named Most Valuable Player in the league by both the baseball writers and by his fellow American Leaguers. He would have been a unanimous choice by the players if the rules did not disallow teammates to vote for a man on their own club. Dick Williams, his manager, said simply: "He was a perfect player for me."

In the World Series that followed, Yastrzemski was as responsible as any Boston player for grittily carrying the Cardinals to a full seven-game set. He batted .400, including three home runs and five runs-batted-in. He covered left field brilliantly, making sixteen putouts (some of them in the spectacular category) and threw out two of the speedy Cardinals who tried to run on his vaunted arm.

Yet his greatest days in baseball must remain those two fantastic set-tos that climaxed the 1967 season. In Boston they called it The Year of Yastrzemski.

CY YOUNG

as told to Francis J. Powers

There's just no competition, Denton True "Cy" Young is too far ahead! Born March 29, 1867, in Gilmore, Ohio, Cy pitched 22 years for five clubs in both majors and hung up more victories, 511, and pitched more games, 906, than any pitcher in history. He tossed three no-hitters, just about par for the course. Young died in 1955.

A PITCHER'S got to be good and he's got to be lucky to get a no-hit game. But to get a perfect game, no run, no hit, no man reach first base, he's got to have everything his way. There have been only seven perfect games pitched in the big leagues since 1880.

I certainly had my share of luck in the 23 years I pitched in the two big leagues because I threw three no-hitters and one of them was perfect. You look at the records and you'll find that Larry Corcoran, who pitched for the Chicago Nationals "away back when," was the only other big leaguer ever to get three no-hitters and none of them was perfect.

So it's no job for me to pick out my greatest day in baseball. It was May 5, 1904, when I was pitching for the Boston Red Sox and beat the Philadelphia Athletics without a run, hit or man reaching first. I'll be 78 next month, but of all the 879 games I pitched in the big leagues that one stands clearest in my mind.

The American League was pretty young then, just four seasons old, but it had a lot of good players and good teams.

185

I was with St. Louis in the National when Ban Johnson organized the American League and I was one of the many players who jumped to the new circuit.

Jimmy Collins, whom I regard as the greatest of all third basemen, was the first manager of the Boston team and in 1903 we won the pennant and beat Pittsburgh in the first modern World Series.

Before I get into the details of my greatest day, I'd like to tell something about our Red Sox of those days. We had a great team. Besides Collins at third we had Freddie Parent at short, Hobe Ferris at second and Candy La Chance on first. You find some real old-timer and he'll tell you how great those fellows were.

In the outfield were Buck Freeman, who was the Babe Ruth of that time, Patsy Dougherty, who later played with the White Sox and Chick Stahl. Bill Dineen was one of our other pitchers and he'd licked the Pirates three games in the world's series the fall before.

Every great pitcher usually has a great catcher, like Mathewson had Roger Bresnahan and Miner Brown had Johnny Kling. Well, in my time I had two. First, "Chief" Zimmer, when I was with Cleveland in the National League, and then Lou Criger, who caught me at Boston and handled my perfect game.

As I said, my greatest game was against the Athletics, who were building up to win the 1905 pennant, and Rube Waddell was their pitcher. And I'd like to say that beating Rube anytime was a big job. I never saw many who were better pitchers.

I was real fast in those days but what very few batters knew was that I had two curves. One of them sailed in there as hard as my fast ball and broke in reverse. It was a narrow curve that broke away from the batter and went in just like a fast ball. And the other was a wide break. I never said much about them until after I was through with the game.

There was a big crowd for those times out that day. Maybe 10,000, I guess, for Waddell always was a big attraction.

I don't think I ever had more stuff and I fanned eight, getting Davis and Monte Cross, Philly shortstop, twice. But the boys gave me some great support and when I tell you about it, you'll understand why I say a pitcher's got to be awfully lucky to get a perfect game.

The closest the Athletics came to a hit was in the third

when Monte Cross hit a pop fly that was dropping just back of the infield between first and second. Freeman came tearing in from right like a deer and barely caught the ball.

But Ollie Pickering, who played center field for Mr. Mack, gave me two bad scares. Once he hit a fly back of second that Chick Stahl caught around his knees after a long run from center. The other time Ollie hit a slo wroller to short and Parent just got him by a step.

Patsy Dougherty helped me out in the seventh when he crashed into the left field fence to get Danny Hoffman's long foul; and I recall that Criger almost went into the Boston bench to get a foul by Davis.

Most of the other batters were pretty easy but all told there were 10 flies hit, six to the outfield. The infielders had seven assists and I had two and 18 of the putouts were divided evenly between Criger and La Chance.

Well, sir, when I had two out in the ninth, and it was Waddell's time to bat, some of the fans began to yell for Connie Mack to send up a pinch hitter. They wanted me to finish what looked like a perfect game against a stronger batter.

But Mr. Mack let Rube take his turn. Rube took a couple

THE BOX SCORE
(May 5, 1904)

BOSTON	A.B.	R.	H.	P.	A.	ATHLETICS	A.B.	R.	H.	P.	A.
Dougherty, lf.	4	0	1	1	0	Hartsel	1	0	0	0	0
Collins, 3b.	4	0	2	2	0	Hoffman, lf.	2	0	0	2	1
Stahl, cf.	4	1	1	3	0	Pickering, cf.	3	0	0	1	0
Freeman, rf.	4	0	1	2	0	Davis, 1b.	3	0	0	5	0
Parent, ss.	4	0	2	1	4	L. Cross, 3b.	3	0	0	4	1
La Chance, 1b.	3	0	1	9	0	Seybold, rf.	3	0	0	2	0
Ferris, 2b.	3	1	1	0	3	Murphy, 2b.	3	0	0	1	2
Criger, c.	3	1	1	9	0	M. Cross, ss.	3	0	0	2	3
Young, p.	3	0	0	0	2	Schreck, c.	3	0	0	7	0
						Waddell, p.	3	0	0	0	1
Totals	32	3	10	27	9	Totals	27	0	0	24	8

	1	2	3	4	5	6	7	8	9	
ATHLETICS	0	0	0	0	0	0	0	0	0	0—0
BOSTON	0	0	0	0	0	1	2	0	x	—3

Error—Davis. Two-base hits—Collins, Criger. Three-base hits—Stahl, Freeman, Ferris. Sacrifice hit—La Chance. Left on bases—Boston 5. Double plays—Hoffman to Schreck, L. Cross to Davis. Struck out—By Young 8, Waddell 6. Time—1:23. Umpire—Dwyer. Attendance —10,267.

of strikes and then hit a fly that Stahl caught going away from the infield.

You can realize how perfect we all were that day when I tell you the game only took one hour and 23 minutes.

We got three runs off Waddell and when the game was finished it looked like all the fans came down on the field and tried to shake my hand. One gray-haired fellow jumped the fence back of third and shoved a bill into my hand. It was $5.

The game was a sensation at the time. It was the first perfect game in 24 years, or since 1880, when both John M. Ward and Lee Richmond did the trick. It also was the second no-hitter ever pitched in the American League. Jimmy Callahan of the White Sox pitched the first against Detroit in 1902 but somehow a batter got to first base.

During my 23 years in the big leagues I pitched 472 games in the National League and won 291, and then I went into the American League and won 220 there. So all told I worked 879 games and won 511 and far as I can see these modern pitchers aren't gonna catch me.

By the way, you might be interested to know that in my last big-league game I was beaten 1–0 by a kid named Grover Cleveland Alexander.